SEED BEAD **FUSION**

SEED BEAD **FUSION**

18 PROJECTS TO STITCH, WIRE & STRING

RACHEL **NELSON-SMITH**

interweavestore.com

EDITOR Jean Campbell
COVER & INTERIOR DESIGN Pamela Norman
PHOTOGRAPHY Joe Coca
STEP PHOTOGRAPHY Rachel Nelson-Smith
PHOTO DIRECTOR Connie Poole
PHOTO STYLING Ann Swanson
TECHNICAL EDITOR Jean Campbell
ILLUSTRATIONS Rachel Nelson-Smith
PRODUCTION DESIGNER Katherine Jackson

Interweave Press LLC
201 East Fourth Street
Loveland, CO 80537-5655 USA
interweavestore.com

Printed in China by Asia Pacific Offset.

Library of Congress
Cataloging-in-Publication Data

Nelson-Smith, Rachel.
 Seed bead fusion : 18 projects to stitch, wire, and string /
Rachel
Nelson-Smith.
    p. cm.
 Includes bibliographical references and index.
 ISBN 978-1-59668-156-9 (pbk.)
1. Beadwork. 2. Jewelry making. I. Title.
 TT860.N46 2009
 745.58'2--dc22

                            2009008797

10 9 8 7 6 5 4 3 2

CONTENTS

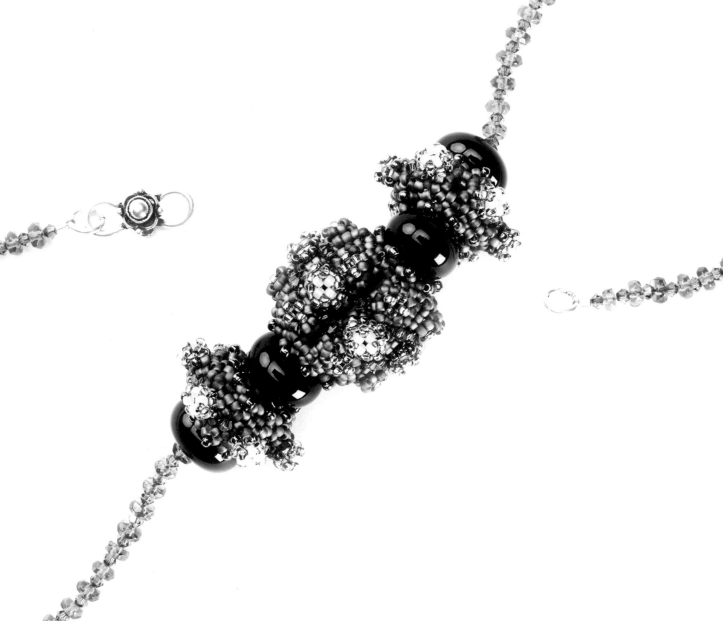

Welcome to *Seed Bead Fusion*, where you have a chance to mix and match beadweaving, wireworking, and stringing techniques for your beading pleasure. I encourage you to try these projects on for size one by one and enjoy the exploration of merging stitches and changing techniques. Whether you're new to jewelry making or been at it a while, there is a design here for you.

Why mix and match techniques? Having worked in several bead stores, I answered a lot of questions about beading and, honestly, I've seen more funky jewelry that one ought to see. From answering questions that cover everything from stringing to beadweaving to wireworking, a desire grew in me to approach the same techniques a little differently by adding seed beads to wire or merging one beadweaving stitch into another. And, from making my own ill-fated beadwoven pieces to seeing mis-stitched pieces that I know were bound to fall apart, I've learned that reinforcing beadwork with wire is an invaluable technique for strengthening and prolonging a piece of jewelry's lifespan.

How to Use This Book

You'll find that in each project I've presented "Rachel's Tips": Little techniques I share that will help your project go more smoothly. I've also included "What's the Story"—tales about the kernels of creativity that inspired each project. Just about all the projects feature clear color illustrations, and I'm really excited to share the multiple step-by-step photos. While many steps for each project are covered within the directions, information on bead stitches, wireworking, and general jewelry making is included in the Basics section. Some of my favorite materials are noted here, too. Finally, please note that I've made just about each project in multiple colorways. Take my lead and create projects that are uniquely your own.

So, I encourage you to think about beaded and wire-jewelry-making techniques a little differently. Add a little bit of something unusual, perhaps causing a happy accident. Trust me, even *Ootheca Cuff* (page 8) was born out of a series of trying something new and being unafraid to make a mistake. I also encourage you to widen your beading abilities and learn more techniques. The more techniques you learn, the more creative possibilities there are.

I hope you enjoy these pieces designed to dazzle you. Think big and have a great time. I look forward to seeing what you come up with!

Rachel

Combine right-angle weave, tubular peyote stitch, and a little basic wireworking to create this stunning cratered double-sided cuff.

WHAT'S THE STORY?

This cuff design arrived one night while I was watching a DVD with my husband. Out of the blue, he wanted to work on a beading project, too. After setting him up with a peyote brace-let project, I wondered what my own project would be. The memory of a man's bracelet I'd seen years earlier popped into my mind—an image that haunted me since I'd first seen it. In my endeavor to watch the movie, help with Colin's project, and create my own, my cuff design came out considerably different than planned! Having worked several rows, I real-ized the cuff had amazing dimension, much like an egg crate. Thus "Ootheca" (Latin for an insect's egg case) was born.

TECHNIQUES
Attaching jump rings
Head pin
Right-angle weave
Tubular peyote stitch
Basic loop
See pages 122–140 for helpful technique information.

MATERIALS
80 g opaque lavender size 11°
    Japanese seed beads (A)
15 g sapphire luster size 11°
    Japanese seed beads (B)
320 amethyst 2AB 3mm
    crystal bicones
3 silver 6mm round
    magnetic clasps
16 sterling silver 4mm
    jump rings
Gray or smoke beading thread
14' (4.3m) of sterling silver
    22-gauge round wire

TOOLS
Size 12 beading needle
Thread snips or small
    scissors
Fine-point permanent marker
Flush wire cutters
Wire straighteners
2 pairs of chain-nose pliers
Round-nose pliers

SIZING
You can size this bracelet to fit
    your wrist by adding length
    to the base:
SMALL 27 units long
MEDIUM 29 units long
LARGE 31 units long

Note The base length should
always be an odd number of
units. If you're unsure of the
length, make each base band
two rows shorter than you
think you need. More units can
be added later.

1 BASES. Use 6' (1.8m) of single thread to right-angle weave a band:

Row 1, Unit 1 String 16A, leaving a 6" (15.2cm) tail. Tie a knot to form a tight circle. Pass through the first 4A (FIGURE 1).

Row 1, Unit 2 String 12A and pass through the 4A you last exited from the previous unit and the first 8A just added (FIGURE 2).

Row 1, Units 3-6 Repeat Row 1, Unit 2 four times (FIGURE 3). Pass through the top 4A of the final unit to step up to the next row.

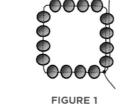

FIGURE 1

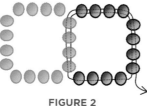

FIGURE 2

FIGURE 3

Row 2 String 12A and pass through the 4A last exited and the first 4A just added (FIGURE 4). String 8A and pass through the top 4A of the next unit from the previous row, the 4A last exited in the previous unit, the 8A just added, and the top 4A of the following unit from the previous row (FIGURE 5). Repeat, working right-angle weave across the row to complete a total of 6 units.

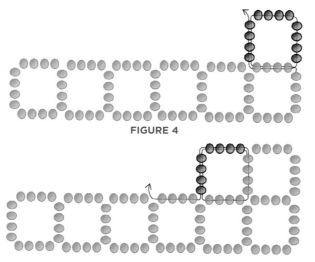

FIGURE 4

FIGURE 5

RACHEL'S TIPS

→ Even though it's tempting to jump ahead in the instructions, you'll find it's considerably easier to stitch the bracelet together if you complete both sides of the embellished base first.

→ Coat your thread with beeswax to help maintain thread tension.

→ Use a fair amount of thread tension as you work. It will help clarify where the next bead should be added. Don't overdo the tension, though, as the overall "stiffness" of the cuff will increase when the wirework binding is added.

→ When beading the bumps it may help you keep track of your place if you pile the number of beads required for each round in an ice cube tray or other separator.

→ This cuff is reversible, so consider making the sides different in contrasting or complementing colors. There are many wonderful variations to choose from.

Rows 3-end Repeat Row 2 to the desired base size (see *Note* on bottom of page 9). Secure the thread and trim. Set aside. Repeat this step to make a second base.

2 BUMPS. Start a new thread on one of the bases that exits from 3A at the bottom of the first unit in Row 1. Use A beads to weave tubular peyote stitch "bumps" on the surface of the bases.

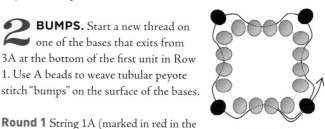

FIGURE 6

Round 1 String 1A (marked in red in the photos on page 13) and pass through the middle 2A of the next side in the unit; repeat 3 times to add 1A to each corner of the unit. Step up for the next round by passing through the first 1A added in this round (FIGURE 6).

Round 2 String 2A (yellow in photos) and pass through the next 1A from Round 1; repeat 3 times. Step up through the first 2A added in this round (FIGURE 7).

Round 3 String 1A (blue in photos) and pass through the next 2A from Round 2; repeat 3 times. Step up through the first 1A added in this round (FIGURE 8).

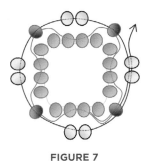

FIGURE 7

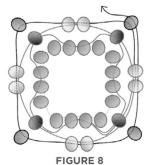

FIGURE 8

Round 4 String 1B (white in photos) and pass through the next 1A from Round 3; repeat 3 times. Step up through the first 1B added in this round (FIGURE 9). To assist in tension, step down to 1A of Row 3 and step back up to 1B of Row 4. Pass through the 4B added in this round to close the bump. Weave through the beads to exit from 3A at the bottom of the third unit in the row.

Repeat this step to embellish every other unit on the base so it resembles a checkerboard. Secure the thread and trim.

Repeat with the second base, this time starting with the second unit in Row 1 so that the two bases end up mirroring each other (FIGURE 10).

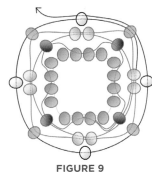

FIGURE 9

FIGURE 10

3 **ASSEMBLY.** Bring the flat sides of the bases together so that Row 1 on the first base lines up with Row 2 on the second base. This will fill all the openings in the bases with bumps as well as provide a "ledge" to place the clasps (FIGURE 11).

Start a new thread that exits from 4A at the side of Row 1 on the first base. String 1A and pass through the adjacent 4A of Row 2 on the second base. String 1A and pass through the original 4A, the first 1A just added, and the next 4A on the second base. Repeat along the edges, connecting the two bases with right-angle weave units (FIGURE 12).

FIGURE 11

FIGURE 12

4 **CLASPS.** Mark the edge of each clasp half with a vertical line on both sides to indicate the thread path for the clasp loop. These lines will serve as a guide when you stitch the clasps in place (FIGURE 13).

Weave the working thread to exit down through 1B in a Round 4, Row 1 bump on the first base. String 1 clasp and pass through the 1B on the other side of Round 4. Pull tight so the clasp pulls inside the bump. Repeat the thread path 6 or more times to reinforce. Repeat to add 1 clasp to each empty bump at the end of the bracelet. Separate the clasps and stitch the remaining halves to the bumps on the other end of the bracelet.

FIGURE 13

5 **WIRE BINDING.** Form a head pin bend at the end of the wire. String 1 bicone and pass the bare wire through both base layers where 4 right-angle weave units meet. String 1 bicone and flush cut the wire about ⅛" (3mm) above the bead. Form another head-pin bend to secure the beads and wire in place.

Repeat this step to bind each row of the cuff with 5 beaded head pins.

6 SAFETY CHAIN. Use the wire to make 7 beaded links with 1 bicone each; set aside. Use 2 jump rings to attach 1 beaded link to an open right-angle-weave unit at the corner of the bracelet. Use 2 jump rings to attach the link just placed to another link; repeat to make a chain of beaded links. Use 2 jump rings to attach the end of the chain to the open right-angle-weave unit at the other end of the bracelet.

Ootheca Cuff—"Cook" variation

Ootheca Cuff— "Mandarine" variation

OOTHECA at-a-glance

1 Bumps, Round 1 step up

2 Bumps, Round 2 step up

3 Bumps, Round 3 step up

4 Bumps, Round 4 step up

5 Bumps, close the bump

6 Bases

7 Base line-up

8 Base edge binding with right-angle weave

9 Mark the clasp

10 Clasp pulled inside a bump

11 Binding with beaded head pins

12 Head-pin bend

Cover a round bead with peyote stitch, then embellish to create as sturdy a finish as a cancan dancer at the end of a long evening.

WHAT'S THE STORY?

My parents requested a special present to commemorate my Aunt Mary's fiftieth birthday. After quite a bit of mis-stitching with odd increases and decreases, a symmetrical pattern emerged, and a flirty pair of earrings was born.

TECHNIQUES
Attaching ear wires
Tubular peyote stitch
Ending and starting thread
Wrapped loop
Wrapped bead link
Briolette wrap
See pages 122–140 for helpful technique information.

MATERIALS
2 clear 8mm Czech druk beads
1 g black size 11° seed beads
1 g white size 11° seed beads
3 g red 3.4mm drop beads
16 light Siam AB 4mm crystal sequins
16 black size 15° seed beads
2 jet 6x13mm crystal briolettes
8" (20.3cm) of sterling silver 22-gauge dead-soft round wire
6" (15.2cm) of sterling silver 24-gauge dead-soft round wire
Gray or smoke beading thread

TOOLS
Flush cutters
Chain-nose pliers
Round-nose pliers
Size 12 beading needles
Thread snips or small scissors
Wire straighteners

FINISHED SIZE
1.75" (4.5 cm)

RACHEL'S TIPS

→ Make sure to go through the last round of eight beads to secure them before going on to embellish. This will ensure the last beads sit snug and tidy around the wirework stem.

→ Coating the thread in beeswax will help maintain tension.

→ A fair amount of tension simplifies this beading process and makes clearer where the next bead should be added. A good way to maintain tension is by giving the thread a slight tug after the addition of each bead.

→ Make a necklace by linking many beaded beads rosary-chain style using double jump-ring connections. Finish with a clasp set.

1 BASE BEAD. Cut 4" (10.2cm) of 22-gauge wire and form a 3mm wide wrapped loop at one end. String 1 druk and form another wrapped loop to secure it.

2 BEADED BASE. Use 4' (1.2m) of single thread and size 11's to work tubular peyote stitch over the base bead, following FIGURE 1.

Round 1 String 8 black and tie a square knot to form a tight ring. Place the ring over one of the base bead's wrapped loops. Pass through the first bead strung to hide the knot.

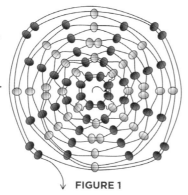

FIGURE 1

Round 2 String 1 white and pass through the next 2 Round 1 beads; repeat to add a total of 4 beads. Step up for the next round by passing through the first bead added in this round.

Round 3 String 1 black, 1 white, and 1 black and pass through the next Round 2 bead; repeat to add a total of 12 beads. Step up through the first 3 beads added in this round.

Round 4 String 1 white and pass through the next Round 3 three-bead sequence; repeat to add a total of 4 beads. Step up through the first bead added in this round.

Round 5 String 1 black and pass through the middle white in the next sequence from Round 3, then string 1 black and pass through the following Round 4 white; repeat to add a total of 8 black. Step up through the first bead added in this round.

Round 6 String 2 white and pass through the next Round 5 black, then string 1 white and pass through the following Round 5 black; repeat to add a total of 12 white. Step up through the first 2 beads added in this round.

Round 7 String 1 black and pass through next 1 Round 6 white, then string 1 black and pass through the following 2 Round 6 whites; repeat to add a total of 8 black. Step up through the first bead added in this round.

Round 8 String 1 white and pass through the next Round 7 black; repeat around to add a total of 8 white. Step up through first bead added in this round.

Round 9 String 1 black and pass through the next Round 8 white; repeat to add a total of 8 black. Step up through first bead added in this round.

Round 10 Without adding a bead, pass through the next Round 9 black to make a decrease, then string 1 white and pass through the following Round 9 black; repeat to add a total of 4 white. Step up through first bead added in this round.

Round 11 String 2 black and pass through next Round 10 white; repeat to add a total of 8 black. Pass through all of the beads added in this round 2 times and pull tight.

3 FRINGE. Slide the needle down the thread toward the beadwork so you can work with doubled thread. Exiting Round 11 of the beaded bead, work rounds of fringe:

Round 1 String 1 drop and pass through the next 2 Base Round 11 beads; repeat to add a total of 4 drops.

Round 2 Weave through beads to exit Base Round 9. String 1 drop and pass through the next Base Round 9 bead; repeat to add a total of 8 drops.

Round 3 Weave through beads to exit either 1 white or 2 whites in Base Round 6. String 1 sequin and 1 size 15° and pass back through the sequin and the following Base Round 6 stitch; repeat around to add a total of 8 sequins.

Rounds 4 and 5 Repeat Fringe Rounds 1 and 2 in reverse to embellish Base Rounds 1 and 3 on the beaded bead.

4 ASSEMBLY. Cut 3" (7.6cm) of 24-gauge wire. Use the wire and 1 briolette to form a briolette dangle that attaches to the bottom wrapped loop of the beaded bead. Use chain-nose pliers to attach an ear wire to the top loop.

Repeat all to make the second earring.

CANCAN at-a-glance

① Base, Round 2 step up

② Base, Round 3, first stitch

③ Base, Round 4, first stitch

④ Base, Round 5, first stitch

⑤ Base, Round 5, second stitch

⑥ Base, Round 6, first stitch

⑦ Base, Round 6, second stitch

⑧ Base, Round 7, first stitch

⑨ Base, Round 7, second stitch

⑩ Base, Round 8 step up

⑪ Base, Round 9, first stitch

⑫ Base, Round 10 step up

⑬ Base, Round 11

⑭ Fringe, Round 1, first fringe

⑮ Fringe, Round 2, first fringe

⑯ Fringe, Round 3, first fringe

An embellished quadruple helix rope with a tubular peyote-stitched start becomes a wearable sea of beads.

WHAT'S THE STORY?

As a nineteen-year-old beadweaving whelp working for the first time in a bead shop, customer Marcia DeCoster once astounded me with the beadworked necklace she wore. My jaw dropped. True to her word, she brought directions for the stitch on her next visit. Eventually, I taught my variation of the project as *Embellished African Helix Bracelet* which was a fun project but always difficult to start. Finally after over a decade of working with this stitch, I discovered a surefire way to start the helix: begin it with another easier stitch!

TECHNIQUES
Attaching jump rings
Head pin
Wrapped loop
Quadruple helix
Peyote stitch
See pages 122–140 for helpful technique information.

MATERIALS
10 g nickel-plated size 11°
    seed beads (A)
60 g silver-lined blue AB size
    11° seed beads (B)
20 g crystal AB size 11°
    seed beads (C)
30 g crystal AB size 6°
    seed beads (D)
2 clear 8mm Czech glass
    round beads
2 sterling silver 5mm
    18-gauge jump rings
1 sterling silver toggle clasp
Gray or smoke beading thread
8" (20.3cm) of sterling silver
    22-gauge dead-soft round
    wire

TOOLS
2 pairs of chain-nose pliers
Round-nose pliers
Wire cutters
Size 12 beading needles
Thread snips or small scissors
Wire straighteners

FINISHED SIZE
Necklace 19½" (49.5cm)
Bracelet 9¼" (23.5cm).
Note The bracelet's larger-than-normal measurement is necessary because of the rope's diameter. The bracelet shown on page 19 fits a 6½" (16.5cm) wrist.

1 **ANCHOR BEADS.** Cut 4" (10.2cm) of 22-gauge wire and form a head pin at one end. String 1 glass round bead and form a wrapped loop to secure it. Repeat to make a second anchor bead. Set aside.

2 **BEAD CAP.** Use a working length of single thread and A to cover the anchor beads with tubular peyote stitch (FIGURE 1):

Round 1 String 8A, leaving a 6"(15.2cm) tail. Tie a square knot to form a tight ring; pass through the first bead added in this round. Place the ring over one of the anchor bead's wrapped loops.

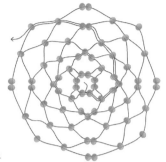

FIGURE 1

Round 2 String 1A and pass through the next 2A of Round 1; repeat to add a total of 4A. Step up by passing through first bead added in this round.

Round 3 String 3A and pass through the next 1A from Round 2; repeat to add a total of 12A. Step up through first 3 beads added in this round.

Round 4 String 1A and pass through the next 3A from Round 3; repeat 3 more times to add a total of 4A. Step up through first bead added in this round.

Round 5 String 1A and pass through the middle bead of the next 3A set from Round 3, then string 1A and pass through the next 1A from Round 4; repeat to add a total of 8A. Step up through first bead added in this round.

Round 6 String 2A and pass through the next 1A from Round 5, then string 1A and pass through the next 1A from Round 5; repeat to add a total of 12A. Step up through the first 2 beads added in this round.

Round 7 String 1A and pass through the next 1A from Round 6, then string 1A and pass through the next 2A from Round 6; repeat to add a total of 8A. Step up through the first bead added in this round.

Rounds 8 and 9 Repeat Rounds 6 and 7. Secure the thread and trim. Set aside.

Repeat this step to cover the second anchor bead; don't trim the thread.

3 **HELIX BASE.** Use the tail thread on the second bead cap to work one round of netting, then work quadruple helix to form a rope.

Round 1 String 3B, 1A, and 1B and pass through the next 1A of Round 9; repeat to add four 5-bead loops.

Round 2 String 3B, 1A, and 1B and slide the beads to the base. Pass the needle between (not through) the first 3B and 1A from the previous round from the outside to the inside. This new 5-bead loop is added by hooking the thread rather than actually stitching through any beads. Remove any slack by pulling on the working thread and make sure the new 5-bead loop is in the correct place as shown in FIGURE 2.

Rounds 3 and on Repeat Round 2 to add 5-bead loops until you reach the desired length minus the length of the remaining bead cap and clasp.

Final Base Round String 3B and pass through 1A in Round 9 of the second bead cap (FIGURE 3), then string 1B and loop around the next 5-bead loop of the helix as before (FIGURE 4); repeat 3 more times to completely attach the anchor to the base. Repeat this thread path again to firmly secure the helix to the cap. Weave in the thread and trim.

FIGURE 2

FIGURE 3

FIGURE 4

4. **WAVES.** Make waves by embellishing the four spiraling spines of the quadruple helix with 6 rows of peyote stitch and 2 rows of three-drop netting. Follow FIGURE 5 for bead counts and color placement:

Row 1 Start a new length of working thread that exits from the first 1A of a spine on the helix. String 1B and pass through the next 1A on the same spine. Repeat down the spine until you reach the last 1A.

Row 2 String 1B and pass back through the next 1B from Row 1, making a turnaround. Repeat down the row to the second 1B added in Row 1.

Row 3 String 1B and pass back through the next 1B from Row 2, then string 2B and stitch through the next 1B from Row 2. Repeat, alternating stitches down the row to the second 1B added in Row 2. *Note:* Depending on the length of your bracelet, you may end Row 3 by adding 2B or 1B.

Row 4 String 1B and pass back through the next 1B from Row 3. String 1B and pass back through the next 2B from Row 3. Repeat down the row to the second bead(s) added in Row 3. *Note:* You will end Row 4 by stitching through 1B or 2B in Row 3.

Row 5 String 2B and pass back through 1B from Row 4, then string 1B and stitch through 1B from Row 4. Repeat down the row to the second 2B added in Row 4.

Row 6 String 1C and pass back through 2B from Row 5, then string 1C and pass back through 1B from Row 5. Repeat down the row to the second bead(s) added in Row 5.

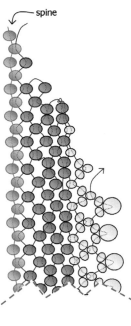

spine

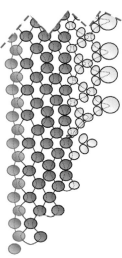

FIGURE 5

Row 7 Weave back through the beads to exit the second-to-last C added in Row 6. String 3C and pass back through the next 1C (FIGURE 6). Repeat down the row to the second bead added in Row 6.

Row 8 Weave back through the beads to exit the middle 1C of the second-to-last 3C set added in Row 7. String 1C, 1D, and 1C and pass back through the middle 1C of the next 3C set (FIGURE 7). Repeat down the row to the second 3C set added in Row 7.

Weave through the beadwork to exit from the first 1A of the next spine on the helix. Repeat Rows 1–8 to add one wave to each spine.

For a very full piece, you may add a second wave to the same helix spine. Just pass through the beadwork to exit 1A at the end of a spine. String 1B and pass through next 1A of the spine. Repeat to the end of the spine. Continue to create in the same manner as other waves.

FIGURE 6

FIGURE 7

PACIFIC WAVES
at-a-glance

1 Bead Cap, Round 2, first stitch

2 Bead Cap, Round 3, first stitch

3 Bead Cap, Round 4, first stitch

4 Bead Cap, Round 5, first stitch

5 Bead Cap, Round 5, second stitch

6 Bead Cap, Round 6, first stitch

7 Bead Cap, Round 6, second stitch

8 Bead Cap, Round 7, first stitch

9 Bead Cap, Round 7, second stitch

10 Bead Cap, Round 8, first stitch

11 Bead Cap, Round 8, second stitch

12 Helix base, Round 1, first stitch

13 Helix base, Round 2, first stitch

14 Helix base, Round 2, first loop

15 Last helix base round

16 Final base round, connecting bead cap

17 Final base round, looping back to helix

18 Finished base

19 Waves, Row 1, first stitch

20 Waves, Row 1, last stitch

21 Waves, Row 2, first stitch

22 Waves, Row 3, first stitch

23 Waves, Row 3, second stitch

24 Waves, Row 4, first stitch

25 Waves, Row 4, second stitch

26 Waves, Row 5, first stitch

27 Waves, Row 5, second stitch

28 Waves, Row 7, first stitch

29 Waves, Row 8, first stitch

Work netting over drapery cord, then add a layer of beaded embellishments to create this sumptuous rope necklace.

WHAT'S THE STORY?

Bede in the title of this project is for "bead" or "prayer"; *Chorda* is Latin for cord. The resulting project is a great marriage between my first job as a salesperson in a fabric store and my love of beads.

TECHNIQUES
Attaching jump rings
Flush cutting
Head pin
Wrapped loop
Tubular netting
Coiled S-clasp (optional)
See pages 122–140 for helpful technique information.

MATERIALS
25 g root beer matte AB size 11° seed beads (A)
15 g metallic bronze size 11° seed beads (B)
10 g opaque turquoise size 8° seed beads (C)
8 g two-tone turquoise size 6° seed beads (D)
2 clear 8mm glass round beads
2 gold 18-gauge 6mm jump rings
1 gold 12x44mm S-clasp with 9mm turquoise bead
6" (15.2cm) of 22-gauge dead-soft round wire
Gray or smoke beading thread
20" (50.8cm) of gold lamé ⅜" (9mm) round drapery cord
Transparent tape

TOOLS
2 pairs of chain-nose pliers
Round-nose pliers
Wire cutters
Scissors
Wire straighteners
Size 12 beading needle
Thread snips or small scissors
Ruler or tape measure

FINISHED SIZE
22½" (57.2cm)

1 **ANCHOR BEADS.** Flush cut 4" (10.2cm) of 22-gauge wire and form a head pin. String one 8mm round and form a 4mm wrapped loop to secure it; set aside. Repeat to make a second anchor bead (FIGURE 1).

FIGURE 1

2 **CORD ENDS.** Wrap the cord ends with one layer of transparent tape. Trim the very end of the cord, leaving some transparent tape in place, to create a clean cord end.

3 **BASE.** Use a comfortable length of single working thread and A and B to stitch a netted base around the body of the cord:

Round 1 String {2A and 1B} 8 times, leaving a 6" (15.2cm) tail. Wrap the beads around the cord and tie a square knot to form a circle of 24 beads. Pass through the first 3 beads strung to exit 1B (FIGURES 2–3).

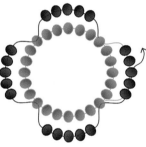

FIGURE 2

Round 2 String 2A, 1B, and 2A, skip 1B in Round 1, and pass through the next 1B; repeat 3 more times to add a total of 4 nets. Step up for the next round by passing up through the first 2A and 1B added in this round (FIGURES 4–5).

FIGURE 3

Round 3 String 2A, 1B, and 2A and pass through the middle 1B of the next net from the previous round; repeat to add a total of 4 nets. Step up the first 2A and 1B added in this round (FIGURE 6).

Rounds 4 and on Repeat Round 3 until you reach the opposite cord end. Work one extra round to extend from the end of the cord; step up through 1B.

Final round String 1A, 1B, and 1A and pass through the middle 1B of the next net in the previous round; repeat to add a total of 4 nets. Step up though 1A and 1B (FIGURE 7).

RACHEL'S TIPS

→ Make your own Coiled S-clasp for this project by following the steps in Basics.

→ When working the base, you may find that the netting appears loose at first, but it will tighten as you add length.

→ The netting tends to bunch up as you work the base, so take a break from stitching every ten rounds to smooth and stretch out the netting.

→ If five-drop netting is a new stitch for you, lay out four piles of 4A and 1B for each round so you'll know how many sections to add and when it is time to step up to the next round.

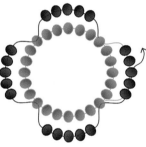

FIGURE 4

FIGURE 5

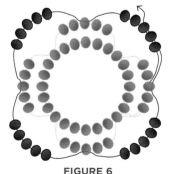

FIGURE 6

FIGURE 7

4. BASE ENDS. Place an anchor bead, looped side out, within the beadwork at the end of the cord (FIGURE 8).

String 1B and pass through middle 1B of the next net; repeat to add a total of 4B (FIGURE 9). Weave through the 4B two times to securely place the anchor bead. Start a new thread at the other base end and repeat.

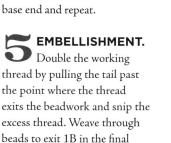

FIGURE 8

5. EMBELLISHMENT. Double the working thread by pulling the tail past the point where the thread exits the beadwork and snip the excess thread. Weave through beads to exit 1B in the final base round. Work rounds of embellishments off the netted base:

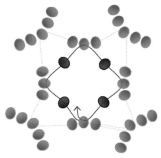

FIGURE 9

Embellishment 1 String 1B, 1C, and 1B and pass through the next 1B in the round, filling the netted opening (FIGURE 10); repeat to add a total of 12 beads. Step up for the next round of embellishment by passing through 2A and 1B of the next netted base round. Repeat to add a total of 6 rounds of embellishment.

Embellishment 2 Weave through beads to exit 1B three rounds down the necklace (FIGURE 11). As you did for Embellishment 1, add 1 round of 1B, 1C, and 1B; step up for the next round by pass-

ing through 2A and 1B of the next netted base round. Work a second round of embellishment using 1B, 1D, and 1B, and a third round using 1B, 1C, and 1B (FIGURE 12). Repeat Embellishment 2 twenty-four more times down the necklace. Repeat Embellishment 1.

6. CLASP. Use jump rings to attach the clasp to the wrapped loops at the ends of the cord.

FIGURE 10

FIGURE 11

FIGURE 12

BEDE CHORDA
at-a-glance

❶ Anchor beads

❷ Taped cord ends

❸ Base, Round 1

❹ Base, Round 2, first stitch

❺ Base, Round 2 step up

❻ Base, Round 3, first stitch

❼ Base, final round, first stitch

❽ Base, final round step up

❾ Base end, anchor bead inserted

❿ Base end, final round's first stitch

⓫ Base end

⓬ Converting to doubled thread

⓭ Embellishment 1, first stitch

⓮ Embellishment 1, first round step up

⓯ Embellishment 2 starting point

16 Embellishment 2, first round step up

17 Embellishment 2, second round step up

18 Embellishment 2, third round step up

Bede Chorda—"Olive Juice" variation

Embellish a three-drop netted base with increasing loop fringe to create a sinuous and textural beaded rope.

WHAT'S THE STORY?

When I finished the embellished three-drop netting for this project, the necklace felt slinky and strong, and the graduated thickness of the embellishments had a fleshy feel. It reminded me of something . . . but what? I realized it was Oola, the beautiful green-skinned creature that danced for Jabba the Hut in the film *Star Wars*. Oola is a Twi'lek who has a pair of lekku, or brain-tails. I imagined the new design was a pair of *Star Wars*–born brain-tails!

TECHNIQUES
Attaching jump rings
Wrapped loop
Tubular peyote stitch
Tubular netting
Coiled S-clasp
See pages 122–140 for helpful technique information.

MATERIALS
25 g metallic bronze size 11° seed beads (A)
100 g transparent light moss size 11° seed beads (B)
140 aqua 6x9mm glass drops (C)
140 turquoise 2XAB 4mm crystal bicones (D)
2 clear 6mm glass round beads
2 gold-filled 5mm 18-gauge jump rings
1 gold-filled 12x34mm S-clasp with rings
4" (10.2cm) of gold-filled 22-gauge round wire
Gray or smoke beading thread

TOOLS
2 pairs of chain-nose pliers
Round-nose pliers
Wire cutters
Wire straighteners
Size 12 beading needles
Thread snips or small scissors

FINISHED SIZE
21¼" (54cm)

RACHEL'S TIPS

→ Use a doubled thread to add the embellishment and to ensure you'll enjoy this necklace for years to come.

→ You may notice the finished necklace is lopsided. You did count correctly! Just gently pull the piece lengthwise in short spans to even things out. This happened to me when finishing up both of the pieces pictured—I thought I had miscounted.

→ Work a shorter length and skip the drop and crystal bead embellishing for a slinky, fringy bracelet.

1 **ANCHOR BEADS.** Cut 4" (10.2cm) of 22-gauge wire and form a head pin at one end. String 1 glass round bead and form a 4mm wrapped loop to secure it. Repeat to make a second anchor bead. Set aside.

2 **BASE ROPE.** Use seed beads to work a tubular netted rope:

Round 1 Use a working length of thread to string 4A, leaving a 6" (15.2cm) tail. Tie a square knot to form a tight ring and pass through the first 1A strung (FIGURE 1). Place the ring over one of the base bead's wrapped loops.

FIGURE 1

Round 2 String 1A and pass through the next bead from Round 1; repeat to add a total of 4A. Step up through the first bead added in this round (FIGURE 2).

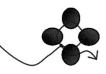

FIGURE 2

Round 3 String 1B, 1A, 1B and pass through the next bead from Round 2; repeat to add a total of 12 beads. Step up through first 2 beads added in this round (FIGURE 3).

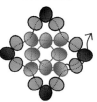

FIGURE 3

Round 4 String 1B, 1A, 1B and pass through the 1A at the center of the next net from the previous round; repeat to add a total of 12 beads. Step up through first 2 beads added in this round (FIGURE 4).

Rounds 5–217 Repeat Round 4 until you've stitched 215 more rounds or your desired length.

Round 218 Insert the second anchor bead into the open end of the netted rope. Exiting from 1A, hold the anchor bead in place as you string 1A and pass through the 1A at the center of the next net from the previous round; repeat to add a total of 4A. Step up through the first bead added in this round. Cinch the last 4A added by passing through them 2 more times. Secure the thread and trim.

FIGURE 4

3 **EMBELLISHMENTS.** Start a new doubled thread that exits from 1A in Base Round 3. Use seed beads, drops, and bicones to work tubular netting embellishments down the length of the base rope:

Rounds 1-10 String 1B, 1A, 1B and pass through the next 1A in the base round you last exited; repeat to add a total of 12 beads. Step up for this (and each subsequent round) by passing through the first 2 beads of the next base round. Repeat this round for a total of 10 rounds.

Round 11 Work as before with 2B, 1A, and 2B in each stitch for a total of 20 beads added to the round.

Rounds 12–21 Alternate Embellishment Rounds 1 and 11 to embellish a total of 10 rounds.

Rounds 22–30 Repeat Embellishment Round 11 for a total of 9 rounds.

Round 31 Work with 3B, 1A, and 3B in each stitch for a total of 28 beads.

Rounds 32–41 Alternate Embellishment Rounds 11 and 31 for a total of 10 rounds.

Rounds 42–50 Repeat Embellishment Round 31 for a total of 9 rounds.

Round 51 Work with 4B, 1A, and 4B in each stitch for a total of 36 beads.

Rounds 52–61 Alternate Embellishment Rounds 31 and 51 for a total of 10 rounds.

Rounds 62–70 Repeat Embellishment Round 51 for a total of 9 rounds.

Round 71 Work with 5B, 1A, and 5B in each stitch for a total of 44 beads.

Rounds 72–81 Alternate Embellishment Rounds 51 and 71 for a total of 10 rounds.

Rounds 82–90 Repeat Embellishment Round 71 for a total of 9 rounds.

Rounds 91–95 Work with 5B, 1A, 1C, 1A, and 5B in each stitch for a total of 52 beads. Repeat this round 4 more times to add a total of 5 rounds.

Rounds 96–100 Work with 5B, 1A, 1D, 1C, 1D, 1A, and 5B in each stitch for a total of 60 beads. Repeat 4 more times to add a total of 5 rounds.

Rounds 101–105 Work with 7B, 1A, 1D, 1C, 1D, 1A, and 7B in each stitch for a total of 76 beads. Repeat 4 more times to add a total of 5 rounds.

Rounds 106–110 Work with 9B, 1A, 1D, 1C, 1D, 1A, and 9B in each stitch for a total of 92 beads. Repeat 4 more times to add a total of 5 rounds.

Repeat this entire step in reverse to embellish the second half of the base.

4 **CLASP.** Use the jump rings to attach the clasp to the anchor beads.

Lekku Necklace—
"Mauve" variation

LEKKU at-a-glance

❶ Base, Round 1

❷ Base, Round 3, first stitch

❸ Base, Round 3 step up

❹ Base, Round 4 step up

❺ Base rope

❻ Base, Round 218, first stitch

❼ Base, Round 218 step up

❽ Embellishment, Round 1, first stitch

❾ Embellishment, Round 1 step up

❿ Embellishment, Round 11, first stitch

⓫ Embellishment, Round 12 step up

⓬ Embellishment, Round 31, first stitch

13 Embellishment, Round 32,
first stitch

14 Embellishment, Round 51,
first stitch

15 Embellishment, Round 71,
first stitch

16 Embellishment, Round 91,
first stitch

17 Embellishment, Round 96,
first stitch

18 Embellishment, Round 101,
first stitch

19 Embellishment, Round 106,
first stitch

This sweet bracelet, with its undulating edges and reversible sides, will put your right-angle weave, tubular peyote stitch, and wireworking skills to task and definitely keep you on your toes!

WHAT'S THE STORY?

While moving the design studio into beautiful downtown Santa Cruz, California, dreams of new designs swirled in my brain. With most of the workshop still in boxes, I sat down and beaded the first iteration of this bracelet in my new workspace. It was aptly named after the studio address on Lincoln Street.

TECHNIQUES
Attaching jump rings
Right-angle weave
Tubular peyote stitch
Basic loop
Head pin
See pages 122–140 for helpful technique information.

MATERIALS
5 g opaque red size 11° seed beads (A)
12 g opaque deep orange size 11° seed beads (B)
4 g opaque yellow size 11° seed beads (C)
5 g opaque grass green size 11° seed beads (D)
12 g opaque cornflower blue size 11° seed beads (E)
4 g opaque lavender size 11° seed beads (F)
3 g opaque orange size 15° seed beads (G)
1 g metallic silver size 15° seed beads (H)
3 g sapphire AB size 15° seed beads (I)
1 g metallic silver size 11° seed beads (J)
6 g hematite 3.4mm Japanese fringe drops
20 jonquil 3mm crystal bicones
20 light amethyst satin 3mm crystal bicones
2 liquid silver 1x4mm tubes
2 sterling silver 4mm 20-gauge jump rings
1 silver 6mm magnetic clasps
Gray or smoke beading thread
2' (61cm) of sterling silver 22-gauge round wire
3" (7.6cm) of sterling silver 2x2.5mm safety chain

TOOLS
2 pairs of chain-nose pliers
Flush cutters
Wire straighteners
Size 12 beading needle
Thread snips or small scissors

FINISHED SIZE
7" (17.8cm)

1 **BASE.** Use a working length of thread and A, B, and C beads to work a base of varying right-angle-weave units. Refer to FIGURE 1 for bead count and color placement:

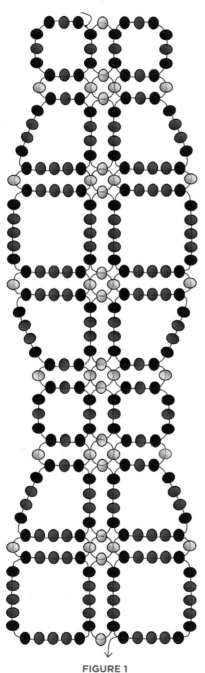

FIGURE 1

RACHEL'S TIPS

→ This bracelet's base incorporates varying right-angle-weave units so the bracelet shape undulates. It can be a challenge to get the units right, so pay extra attention to that portion of the instructions. Otherwise, you'll have beadwork to redo!

→ Once the base is embellished with bumps, the length will contract slightly. The thickness of the beadwork will also make the bracelet shorter. Keep these things in mind as you determine your end length.

→ Repeat rows on each end of the base to make a longer bracelet.

Row 1 String 12 beads; tie a knot to form a tight circle and pass through the first 3 beads just strung. String 5 beads; pass through the 3-bead set last exited and the first 4 beads just strung. String 9 beads; pass through the last 3 beads exited from the previous unit and all of the beads just strung.

Row 2 String 5 beads; pass through the last 3 beads exited and the first bead just strung. String 2 beads; pass through the top bead of the second unit in the previous row, the side bead of the previous unit in this row, the 2 beads just strung, and the 3-bead set at the top of the first unit in the previous row. String 4 beads; pass through the side bead of the previous unit in this row, the 3-bead set last exited, and all the beads just added.

Row 3 String 13 beads; pass through the 3-bead set at the top of the third unit in the previous row and the first 4 beads just added. String 5 beads; pass through the top bead of the second unit in the previous row, the 4-bead set last exited, the 5 beads just added, and the 3-bead set at the top of the first unit of the previous row. String 9 beads; pass through the 4 side beads of the previous unit in this row, the 3-bead set last exited, and the 9 beads just strung.

Row 4 String 7 beads; pass through the 5-bead set at the top of the third unit of the previous row and the first bead just strung. String 2 beads; pass through the top bead of the second unit in the previous row, the side bead of the previous unit in this row, the 2 beads just strung, and the 5-bead set at the top of the first unit in the previous row. String 6 beads; pass through the side bead of the previous unit in this row, the 5-bead set last exited, and all the beads just added.

Row 5 String 15 beads; pass through the 5-bead set at the top of the third unit in the previous row and the first 5 beads just added. String 6 beads; pass through the top bead of the second unit in the previous row, the 5-bead set last exited, the 6 beads just added, and the 5-bead set at the top of the first unit of the previous row. String 10 beads; pass through the 5 side beads of the previous unit in this row, the 5-bead set last exited, and the 10 beads just strung.

Rows 6–10 Repeat Rows 1–4 in reverse; repeat Row 2. The result will be an oval piece of right-angle weave.

Repeat Rows 1–10 four more times to complete the base. Secure the thread and trim. Set aside.

Repeat this step to make a second base using D, E, and F beads.

2 SMALL BUMPS.

Start a new thread on the orange base that exits from the middle bead on one of the sides of the first unit in Row 1. Follow Figure 2 to work tubular peyote-stitched "bumps," referring to the different-colored thread paths for each round (FIGURE 2):

Round 1 (red line) String 1B and pass through the middle bead of the next 3-bead side of the same unit; repeat 3 times. Step up for the next and subsequent rounds by passing through the first bead added in this round.

Round 2 (orange line) String 1G and pass through the next 1G from Round 1; repeat 3 times.

Round 3 (green line) String 1H and pass through the next 1G from Round 2; repeat 3 times (FIGURE 3). Weave through 1G in Round 2 and then pass

FIGURE 2

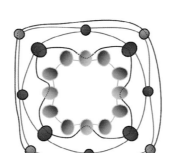

FIGURE 3

through the 4H two times to cinch the beads and close the bump (see blue line in Figure 2).

Weave through the beads to exit from the third unit in Row 1; repeat this step to add another small bump.

3 MEDIUM BUMPS.

Weave through the beads to exit from the middle bead at the top of the first Row 3 unit. Follow FIGURE 4 to work tubular peyote-stitched bumps:

Round 1 (red line) String 1B and pass through the middle 2 beads of the unit's second side. String 1B and pass through the second bead of the unit's third side. String 1B and pass through the fourth bead of the unit's third side. String 1B and pass through the middle 2 beads of the unit's fourth side. String 1B and pass through the middle bead of the unit's first side and step up through the first bead added in this round (FIGURE 5).

Round 2 (orange line) Work in tubular peyote stitch using 1B in each stitch for a total of 5B.

Round 3 (green line) Work in tubular peyote stitch using 1G in each stitch for a total of 5G.

Round 4 (blue line) Work in tubular peyote stitch using 1H in each stitch for a total of 5H. Weave through the next 1G in Round 3 and pass through the 5H from this round 2 times to cinch the beads and close the bump (FIGURE 6).

Weave through the beads to exit from the third unit in Row 3; repeat this step to add another medium bump.

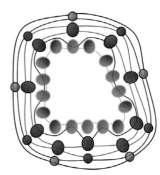

FIGURE 4

FIGURE 5

FIGURE 6

4 LARGE BUMPS.

Weave through the beads to exit from the second bead at the top of the first Row 5 unit. Follow FIGURE 7 to work tubular peyote-stitched bumps:

Round 1 (red line) String 1B, skip 1 bead on the base unit, and pass through the next base bead. String 1B, skip 2 beads on the base unit, and pass through the following base bead. Repeat around to add a total of 8B. Step up for the next and subsequent rounds by passing through the first bead added in this round.

Round 2 (orange line) Work in tubular peyote stitch using 1B in each stitch for a total of 8B.

Rounds 3 and 4 (green and blue lines) Work tubular peyote stitch using 1G in each stitch for a total of 8G in each round.

Round 5 (black line) String 1G; pass through the next 2G of the previous round. Repeat around to add a total of 4G.

Round 6 (pink line) Work in tubular peyote stitch using 1H in each stitch for a total of 4H. Weave through the next 1G in Round 5. Pass through 4H two times to cinch the beads to a point (FIGURE 8; also see brown line in FIGURE 7).

Weave through the beads to exit from the third unit in Row 5; repeat this step to add another large bump.

Repeat Steps 2–4 to embellish the rest of the base with the appropriately sized bumps. Secure the thread and trim. Set aside.

Repeat Steps 2–4 to embellish the blue base, substituting E for B and I for G.

5 EDGES.

Bring the flat sides of the two bases together so they match. Stitch the base edges together with right-angle-weave units:

Unit 1 Start a new thread that exits from the side beads of Row 1 on the orange base, toward the beadwork. String 1J and pass back through the matching side beads of Row 1 on the blue base. String 1J and pass through the Row 1 side beads on the orange base, the first 1J added, the Row 1 side beads on the blue base, and the

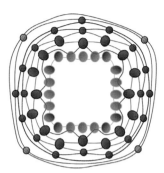

FIGURE 7

FIGURE 8

second 1J added (FIGURE 9).

Unit 2 Pass through the Row 2 side bead at the edge of blue base. String 1J and pass through the Row 2 side bead at the edge of the orange base, and the adjacent 1J added in the previous unit. String 1 drop; pass back through the 1J added in this unit and back through the drop (FIGURE 10). Pass through the 1J added in the previous unit, the drop, and the 1J added in this unit. This figure-eight weaving will securely attach the drop to the unit, keeping it centered.

Repeat Units 1 and 2 along the edges, connecting the two bases with right-angle-weave units; don't add drops to the ends of the bracelet.

FIGURE 9

FIGURE 10

6 CLASP LOOP.

Exit from 1J at the end of the bracelet. String 2J, 1 silver tube, and 2J; pass through the other 1J at the end of the bracelet to form a loop. Repeat the thread path to reinforce. Secure the thread and trim. Repeat this step at the other end of the bracelet. Set aside.

7 WIRE BINDING.

Form a head-pin bend at the end of the wire. String 1 jonquil bicone and pass the bare wire through the second units in Row 2 of both bases, from the orange side to the blue side (FIGURE 11). String 1 amethyst bicone and flush cut the wire about ⅛" (3mm) above the bead. Form another head-pin bend to secure the beads in place.

Repeat this step to bind the bases together at the center of every other row.

FIGURE 11

8 CLASP CHAIN.

Use a jump ring to connect one half of the clasp and one chain end to a clasp loop. Repeat at the other end of the bracelet.

Lincoln Street Bracelet variations
(from left): "Photo (white side),"
"Undergarment (fuchsia side),"
and "Undergarment (blue side)".

LINCOLN STREET
at-a-glance

❶ Bases

❷ Small bump, Round 1 step up

❸ Small bump, Round 2 step up

❹ Small bump, Round 3 step up

❺ Medium bump, Round 1 step up

❻ Medium bump, closing last round

❼ Large bump, closing last round

❽ Edges, Unit 1

❾ Edges, Unit 2, first stitch

❿ Edges, Unit 2, adding drop

⓫ Edges, Unit 2, centering the drop

⑫ Clasp loop

⑬ Wire binding

⑭ Clasp chain

Lincoln Street Bracelet—
"Olive Juice" variation

Explore the vibrant fusion of jewelry making and the colorful influence of Punjabi folk costume while you create a whorl of color and beauty with wire and beads.

WHAT'S THE STORY?

Susan Kazarian of the Beading Frenzy is a trusted friend and idea woman who convinced me the centerpiece of my *Wealwian Curve Necklace* could also work as a bangle. The first one was worked up out of the San Gabriel Bead Company collection in fuchsia, olivine, and blue sparkling crystals reminiscent of wonderfully rich and colorful traditional saris.

TECHNIQUES
Attaching jump rings
Flush cutting
Basic loop
Double basic loop
See pages 122–140 for helpful technique information.

MATERIALS
5 g silver-lined fuchsia size 11° Japanese seed beads

5 g transparent forest green size 8° Japanese seed beads

5 g opaque lime size 6° Japanese seed beads

34 fuchsia 2XAB 4mm crystal bicones

128 jet 2XAB 3mm crystal bicones

19 fuchsia 4mm fire-polished glass rounds

2½' (76.2cm) of sterling silver 18-gauge dead-soft round wire

20' (6.1m) of sterling silver 26-gauge dead-soft round wire

4" (10.2cm) of sterling silver 20-gauge half-hard round wire

2 sterling silver 4mm 20-gauge jump rings

1 sterling silver 4mm 18-gauge jump ring

1 sterling silver 6mm magnetic clasp

3" (7.6cm) of 3mm long-and-short chain

TOOLS
Ruler or tape measure
2 pairs of chain-nose pliers
Round-nose pliers
Flush cutters
Wire straighteners

FINISHED SIZE
7" (17.8cm)

RACHEL'S TIPS

→ The embellishing technique shown with the marquis base is more straightforward than embellishing the centerpiece. While certain beads are called for here, there is a 99% chance your pattern will be different due to the individuality of each marquis component. Always be sure to have an appropriate number of beads filling each space and avoid overfilling.

→ You may find that after you finish embellishing the marquis base or centerpiece base, the ends stick out a little. To remedy, simply trim a small amount of excess from the loop and use round-nose pliers to reform the loop.

→ The various centerpiece base wires will slip around as you try to connect them. Just do your best to keep the frame wires in the correct places. Once the embellishments are added, the frame will stay in place.

→ The centerpiece of this bangle project can also make a beautiful necklace centerpiece. Just make the centerpiece, then finish it off as a necklace with bead-link chain.

2 BEADED WRAPS. Cut a straightened 2' (61cm) piece of 26-gauge wire. Position the wire near one point of the marquis base, leaving a ½" 1.3cm) tail wire. Tightly coil the wire 2 times around the base. Slide the coil so it tucks into one of the base points (**FIGURE 1**).

FIGURE 1

Flip the base over and span the 26-gauge wire across the back. Wrap the 26-gauge wire 2 times around the opposite base wire. String 1 size 11° and wrap the 26-gauge wire around the opposing base wire; span the wire across the back again and form another wrap on the opposite base wire.

String enough 4mm bicones and size 11°, size 8°, and size 6° seed beads to span the space between the base wires. Wrap the 26-gauge wire tightly around the opposite base wire 2 times, span the wire across the bases' back, and form another wrap on the opposite base wire. Continue in this manner to embellish the front of the base. Follow the main project's photo for bead placement or create your own pattern. End by tightly coiling the 26-gauge wire around the base 3 times as you did at the beginning (**FIGURE 2**). Trim the wire close to the wrap if it's too short to continue the edge embellishment.

Note: The marquis shape featured in the photos employs my "Dream" colorway but is done in the same way as for the fuchsia colorway.

FIGURE 2

3 EDGES. String one 3mm bicone on the 26-gauge wire attached to base. Hold the bead in position on the outside of the base as you tightly wrap the 26-gauge wire around the base wire 2 times, between the previous beaded wraps. Continue to add bicones across the edge, keeping the wraps tight against the beads. Repeat to embellish both of the base edges. Trim the wire close to the final wrap. Set the marquis component aside.

1 MARQUIS BASE. Flush cut two 3" (7.6cm) pieces of 18-gauge wire. Form a 3mm double basic loop at one end of each piece. Use your fingers to curve each piece into an arch. Arrange the pieces so they form a marquis shape with one double loop at each end. Slide each looped wire end over the respective non-looped wire end. Form a 3mm basic loop to hold the wires in place. Set aside.

4 CENTERPIECE BASE. Prepare various-size 18-gauge wires and assemble them into a base:
Right wire Flush cut one 6" (15.2cm) piece of 18-gauge wire. Form

a small basic loop at one end of one wire. Use your fingers to curve the wire as in FIGURE 3. Set aside.

Left wire Flush cut one 6" (15.2cm) piece of 18-gauge wire. Form a double basic loop at one end. Use your fingers to curve the wire as in FIGURE 4. Set aside.

Slide the right wire through the coil at the end of the left wire. Use your fingers to curve the wires as necessary so the end result is like FIGURE 5, with the right wire extending to the right and the left wire extending to the left.

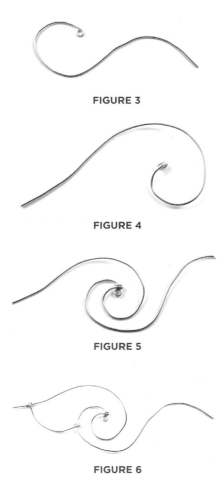

FIGURE 3

FIGURE 4

FIGURE 5

FIGURE 6

Connection wires

Flush cut two 3" (7.6cm) pieces of 18-gauge wire. Form double basic loops at each end of both pieces so that one loop sits on one side of the wire, the other loop on the opposite side. Use your fingers to gently arc the wires. Slide a loop of one of these connection wires onto the end of the right centerpiece wire. Bring up the left centerpiece wire and slide on the second loop, connecting the two centerpiece wires as in FIGURE 6. Form a basic loop at the end of the left centerpiece wire.

Slide the second connection wire onto the right centerpiece wire. Form a simple loop to hold it in place.

5 **CENTERPIECE EMBELLISHMENT.** Fill the centerpiece base with beads and embellish the edges with 3mm bicones the same way you did for the marquis component. Because of the swirling curves the embellishment is more complex, but certainly possible.

Here are a few things to keep in mind as you go:

The exact shape of the unembellished frame is not yet set in stone. As more beads are added you always have the ability to slightly adjust the shape or even take out the last row of beads added. By the midpoint of the embellishing, you'll thread the 26-gauge embellishing wire through previously embellished areas, and this will add to stability.

It's best to use your larger beads, like fire-polished glass, to fill the outside curves of the base since they cover a wider area. Use smaller beads, such as size 11° seed beads, to fill the inside curves where space is limited.

It's best to begin embellishing from the right, then swirl down around to the middle and across the top to the left.

6 **SHAPING.** Use your fingers to gently bend the centerpiece and marquis components in a curve to shape your wrist (FIGURE 7). Use the 5mm jump ring to connect the marquis component to the centerpiece's left side.

FIGURE 7

7 **FINISHING.** Flush cut 2" (5.1cm) of 20-gauge wire. Form a basic loop on one end, string 1 fire-polished bead and form a second basic loop; set aside. Repeat to make a second beaded link. Set aside.

Use a 4mm jump ring to attach one end of a beaded link to the marquis component. Attach one end of the safety chain and half the clasp to the other end of the beaded link. Use a 4mm jump ring to attach one end of the remaining beaded link to the centerpiece component. Attach the remaining end of the safety chain and the other half of the clasp to the other end of the beaded link.

Bhangra Fusion Bangle—
"Noir" variation

BHANGRA FUSION
at-a-glance

❶ Base, curved wires with double loops

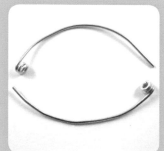

❷ Base, set up for oval shape

❸ Base, shape locked in

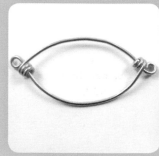

❹ Base, basic loops

❺ Beaded wraps, attachment coil

❻ Beaded wraps, first wire wrap

❼ Beaded wraps, first beaded wrap

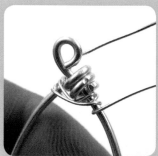

❽ Beaded wraps, second wire wrap across back of base

❾ Beaded wraps, second beaded wrap

❿ Beaded wraps, complete

⓫ Edges, placing first bead

⓬ Edges, five beads placed

13 Centerpiece base, right wire

14 Centerpiece base, left wire

15 Centerpiece base, connected right and left wires

16 Centerpiece base, connection wires double loop orientation

17 Centerpiece base, first connection wire placed

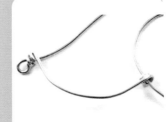

18 Centerpiece base, first connection wire's simple loop

19 Centerpiece base, second connection wire placed

20 Shaping the centerpiece component

Make a strong coiled base and embellish it with thin wire and beads. String the resulting fancy bead into a rich-looking necklace.

WHAT'S THE STORY?

Local Highway 17 winds through beautiful redwood forests of the Santa Cruz Mountains and travels north to south from the bustle of Silicon Valley to the calm of my laid-back coastal town, Santa Cruz. Driving home on this twisting road and thinking over an urgent request for a new project to teach at the upcoming Hooked on Wire retreat, the highway became the inspiration for this project. The remainder of the trip was exciting as I looked forward to sitting down with wire, tools, and beads, which produced the resulting bead that ended up looking more like a butterfly's chrysalis than a highway!

TECHNIQUES
Flush cutting
Crimping
See pages 122–140 for helpful information.

MATERIALS
1' (30.5cm) of copper 18-gauge round wire
6' (1.8m) of copper 26-gauge round wire
4 g bronze metallic size 11° seed beads
3 g root beer silver-lined AB size 11° seed beads
65 amethyst luster 3mm fire-polished glass rounds
6 cranberry 6mm freshwater round pearls
20 peacock 9mm freshwater potato pearls
1 copper 17mm toggle clasp set
2 gold 2x2mm crimp beads
18" (45.7cm) of flexible beading wire

TOOLS
Flush cutters
Ruler or small locking tape measure
Chain-nose pliers
Round-nose pliers
Flat-nose pliers
Crimping pliers
Wire straighteners

FINISHED SIZE
Bead 18x30mm
Necklace 17" (43.2cm)

1 BASE. Use the 18-gauge wire to form a double spiral base:

Z shape Measure 1" (2.5cm) from one end and use chain-nose pliers to form a 90° bend. Repeat at the other wire end to form a Z shape (FIGURE 1).

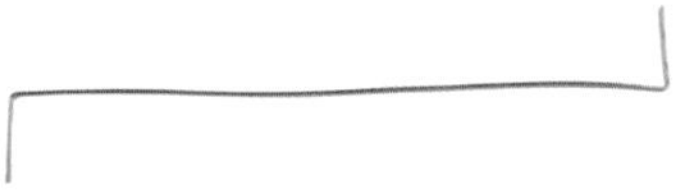

FIGURE 1

U shape Use round-nose pliers to grasp the long section of unbent wire near the bend. Position the pliers so they are parallel to the 1" (2.5cm) tail wire and the jaws grasp at their widest point. Form a 5mm U shape.

Spiral Grasp the U shape in flat-nose pliers. Use your fingers to shape the wire tightly along the U shape; adjust the pliers and repeat to make a flat spiral 3 revolutions wide. Turn the wire over and form another spiral at the other end of the base so that one wire tail points up and the other tail points down. The two spirals should scroll toward one another and each spiral should be about the same size. Use your fingers and chain-nose pliers to continue to spiral the wire until the two spirals are right on top of each other (FIGURE 2).

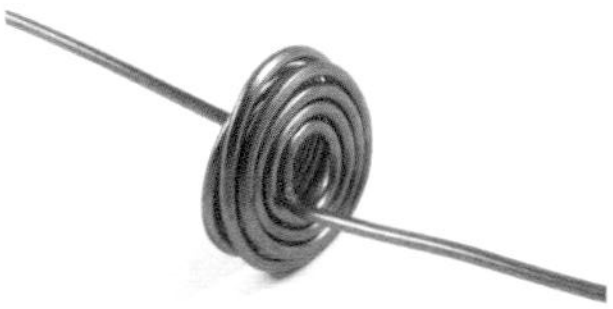

FIGURE 2

Coil Use your fingers or chain-nose pliers to grasp the tail wires. Gently pull the wires apart from each other to form a loose oval coil.

2 EMBELLISHMENT. Use 26-gauge wire and beads to wire-wrap the coiled base:

Attachment Cut a 2' (61cm) length of 26-gauge wire. Tightly wrap the end of the 26-gauge wire around the base near one of the tail wires 2–3 times. Trim any excess 26-gauge wire (FIGURE 3).

FIGURE 3

Round 1 Wrap the 26-gauge wire around the first 2 revolutions of the coiled base. Repeat about 14 times to bind the first 2 spirals into place.

Round 2 String 1 bronze seed bead and lay it between the spiral revolutions. Wrap the 26-gauge wire once around the bottom spiral. Weave to the inside of the coiled base and exit up from the base's top hole and down toward the outside of the base. Repeat to add a total of 14 seed beads (FIGURE 4).

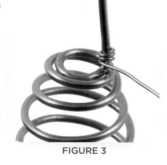

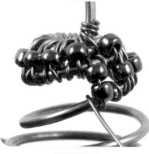

FIGURE 4

Rounds 3 and on Follow the individual wrapping pattern codes on the opposite page while you work these rounds as before in this order: 7 B wraps, 7 C, 1 D, 1 C, 1 D, 1 C, 1 D, 1 E, 1 F, 1 E, 1 D, 1 E, 1 F, 1 E, 1 D, 1 E, 1 F, 1 E, 1 D, 1 E, 1 F, 1 E, 1 D, 1 E, 1 D, 1 E, 1 D, 7 C, 7 B, 14 A. Once you've added the first round of beads, you won't exit up through the coiled base's hole but through the spiral revolution just above (FIGURE 5). ***Note:*** You will run out of 26-gauge wire as you work. See "Adding New Wire" on opposite page to learn how to add more.

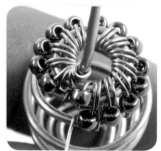

FIGURE 5

Final Beaded Round Repeat Round 2, passing out through the base coil's end hole.

Final Round Repeat Round 1 at the other end of the base coil.

RACHEL'S TIPS

→ I recommend Japanese seed beads for this project because they are not only beautiful, but also fairly uniform.

→ When making the spirals, make sure to press the wire against the pliers' jaws for tidy results.

→ These step-by-step directions can also be used to make a caged bead. Start by making the double-spiraled base but don't embellish it with wire or beads. Instead, make basic loops with the tail wires and pop in an 8mm bead between the spirals. You can also just cut off the tail wires and string right through the oval spiral and inner bead.

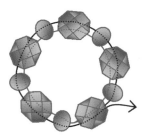

FIGURE 6

FIGURE 7

3 FINISHING. Bend the base coil's tail wire to a 45° angle. Flush cut the tail close to the last wrap, leaving a small amount of wire to help keep the 26-gauge wire from slipping. Set the wire bead aside.

Repeat Steps 1–3 to make a total of 5 beads.

4 SPACERS. Use 8" (20.3cm) of thread to string {1 fire-polished round and 1 bronze size 11°} 4 times. Tie a square knot to form a tight circle and pass through the beads again (FIGURE 6). Tie an overhand knot between beads and pass through the following bead; repeat around the circle (FIGURE 7). Trim the thread close to the beads; set aside. Repeat to make a total of 14 spacers.

5 ASSEMBLY. Use the beading wire to string 1 wire bead. *String {1 spacer, 1 peacock pearl, 1 spacer, and 1 wire bead} 2 times. String 1 spacer, 1 peacock pearl, 1 bronze size 11°, 1 peacock pearl, 1 bronze size 11°, 1 peacock pearl, 1 spacer, 1 cranberry pearl, 1 spacer and 1 peacock pearl. String {1 bronze size 11° and 1 peacock pearl} 4 times. Repeat from * to string the other side of the necklace. Use crimp beads to attach the clasp to the wire ends and cut any excess wire.

WRAPPING PATTERN CODES

A = 1 bronze size 11° seed bead

B = 2 bronze size 11° seed beads

C = 1 bronze size 11° seed bead, 1 root beer size 11° seed bead, and 1 bronze size 11° seed bead

D = 1 bronze size 11° seed bead, 1 fire-polished bead, and 1 bronze size 11° seed bead

E = 1 bronze size 11° seed bead, 2 root beer size 11° seed beads, and 1 bronze size 11° seed bead

F = 1 pearl

ADDING NEW WIRE

Embellishing the wire bead will take more than just the 2' (61cm) piece of 26-gauge you begin with, but it's very difficult to complete the bead with one 6' (1.8m) piece of 26-gauge. Instead, you'll work with smaller increments of wire and add more as needed. Here's how to do it:

When you have difficulty holding onto and manipulating the 26-gauge wire, it's time to change wire. You'll need at least 1½" (3.8cm) of the old working wire to add more. Cut a new 2' (61cm) length of 26-gauge wire and match the end with the end of the old wire. Use your fingers or chain-nose pliers to pinch the two wires and twist them together very tightly several times.

Cut the twisted wires to about ¼" (6mm) and tuck the tail inside the spiral base where it will be out of the way. Resume embellishing as before.

WIRE CHRYSALIS
at-a-glance

❶ Base, Z shape

❷ Base, positioning pliers for U-shape bend

❸ Base, U shape

❹ Base, positioning pliers for spiral

❺ Base, beginning the spiral

❻ Base, spiral continued

❼ Base, double spiral completed

❽ Base, spirals combined

❾ Base, forming the coil

❿ Embellishment, attachment coil

⓫ Embellishment, Round 1, binding the coils

⓬ Embellishment, Round 2, stringing the first bead

⓭ Embellishment, Round 2, making the after-bead wrap

⓮ Embellishment, Round 2, exiting up through top of coiled base

15 Embellishment, Round 2 completed

16 Embellishment, Round 3, first wrap

17 Embellishment, final bead round

18 Embellishment, final round

19 Finishing

Use simple wireworking techniques to create a dazzling pair of earrings that feature a large pearl cradled with wire and embellished with seed beads and crystals.

WHAT'S THE STORY?

The French words for "bead" and "cradle" are *perle* and *berceau*. In this project, precious beads are surrounded by a wire cradle.

TECHNIQUES
Beaded link
Flush cutting
Wrapped loop
Beaded briolette wrap
Attaching ear wires
See pages 122–140 for helpful technique information.

MATERIALS
2 white 12mm crystal pearl rounds
10 sapphire 3mm crystal bicones
12 metallic nickel size 11° seed beads
4 sapphire 11x5.5mm horizontally drilled crystal drops
2 light sapphire 11x5.5mm crystal briolettes
2 sterling silver ear wires
16" (40.6cm) of sterling silver 22-gauge dead-soft round wire
3' (.9m) of sterling silver 26-gauge dead-soft round wire
2' (61cm) of sterling silver 24-gauge dead-soft round wire

TOOLS
3" (7.6cm) piece of scrap 18-gauge wire
Chain-nose pliers
Round-nose pliers
Flush cutters
Wire straightener
Tape measure or ruler

FINISHED SIZE
¾" x 2" (1.9 x 5.1cm)

RACHEL'S TIPS

→ Ensure a smooth cradle by using the wire straightener on the 22-gauge as needed.

→ As the 26-gauge wire embellishing is added, touch the 22-gauge wire only minimally to avoid distortion.

→ Make sure all of the embellishing beads are close to the base wire for a clean result.

Perle Berceau Earrings—
"Rose" variation

1 BASE. Use 8" (20.3cm) of 22-gauge wire and 1 pearl to form a wrapped bead link with 3mm wrapped loops; don't trim the wire on the second loop.

2 CRADLE. Embellish the base with crystal and seed-bead wraps:

Beginning coil Cut a 1½' (45.7cm) piece of 26-gauge wire. Leaving a 1" (2.5cm) tail, tightly wrap the end around the 22-gauge wire 2 times, ¼"(6mm) from the last wrapped loop. Flush cut the 26-gauge tail wire close to the wrap.

Bead wraps (top) Use the 26-gauge wire to string 1 bicone. Hold the bead in position on the outside of the base as you tightly wrap the 26-gauge wire around the 22-gauge wire 2 times. Keep the wraps tight against the bicone. Repeat to add 1 seed bead, 1 seed bead, and 1 bicone.

Loop Hold the scrap 18-gauge wire perpendicular to the 22-gauge wire. Leave the scrap wire in place as you tightly wrap the 26-gauge wire around the base 2 times, creating a loop. Remove the scrap wire.

Bead wrap (bottom) String 1 seed bead; hold the bead in place as you tightly wrap the 26-gauge wire around the 22-gauge wire 2 times; flush cut the 26-gauge tail wire close to the wrap. Slide the 26-gauge wire wraps along the 22-gauge wire toward the second base loop. Re-space the beads as needed to fill the arc between the base's loops. Curve the 22-gauge wire around one side of the pearl. Keep the 22-gauge wire and beads snug against the pearl as you wrap the 22-gauge around the base's first loop 1 time.

Repeat the Bead wrap (top), Loop, and Bead wrap (bottom) steps in reverse to embellish the other half of the pearl; flush cut the

26-gauge tail wire close to the final wrap. Finish by wrapping the 22-gauge 2 times around the base's second wrapped loop; flush cut the 22-gauge tail wire. Use the tip of chain-nose pliers to squeeze in any errant 22-gauge wire.

3 ASSEMBLY. Use 24-gauge wire and a sapphire drop to form a briolette wrap that attaches to one of the cradle 26-gauge loops; repeat for the other loop. Use 24-gauge wire, 1 bicone, and a light sapphire briolette to form a beaded briolette wrap that attaches to the bottom base loop between the 26-gauge loops. Attach an ear wire to the top base loop.

Repeat all steps to create a second earring.

Perle Berceau Earrings—
"Noir" variation

PERLE BERCEAU
at-a-glance

❶ Cradle, beginning coil

❷ Cradle, first bead wrap

❸ Cradle, bead wraps (top)

❹ Cradle, loop

❺ Cradle, bead wraps completed

❻ Cradle, bead wraps curved along the pearl

❼ Cradle, 22-gauge wire bottom wrap

❽ Cradle, final 22-gauge wire wrap

❾ Cradle

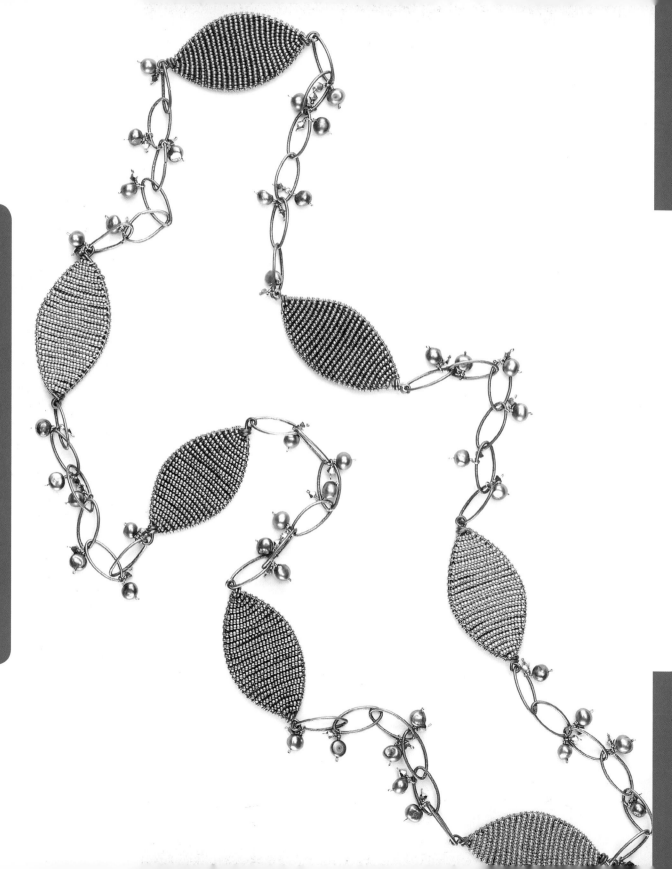

Copper marquis-shaped components are wrapped with beads, linked together with bold chain, and accented by sparkling dangles for a fashion-forward and versatile necklace design.

WHAT'S THE STORY?

When the two perfectly simple 18-gauge wires slipped together to make the first one of these components, I knew the final project would be named after the marquis shape.

TECHNIQUES
Flush cutting
Double basic loop
Wrapped loop
Head pin
See pages 122–140 for helpful technique information.

MATERIALS
12 g sage luster size 15° seed beads (A)
12 g metallic gold size 15° seed beads (B)
42 antique gold 5–6mm freshwater pearls (C)
42 aurum 2X 3mm crystal bicones (D)
4' (1.2m) of copper 18-gauge round wire
46' (14m) of copper 26-gauge round wire
2' (61cm) of copper 7.5x17mm chain

TOOLS
Chain-nose pliers
Round-nose pliers
Flush cutters
Wire straighteners
Ruler

FINISHED SIZE
38" (96.5cm)

→ Consider marking the round-nose pliers' jaws with a permanent marker to help with consistent loop making.

→ Make sure both pieces of 18-gauge are worked in the same manner.

→ Always be sure to have an appropriate number of beads filling each space to avoid overfilling.

1 **BASE.** Flush cut two 3" (7.6cm) pieces of 18-gauge wire and form a 3mm double basic loop at one end of each piece. Use your fingers to curve each piece into an arch. Arrange the pieces so they form a marquis shape with one double loop at each end. Slide each looped wire end over the respective non-looped wire end. Form a 3mm basic loop at each end to hold the wires in place. Set aside.

Repeat to make a total of 7 bases.

2 **BEADED WRAPS.** Cut a 4' (1.2m) piece of 26-gauge wire. Position the wire near the point of one of the bases, leaving a ½" (1.3cm) tail wire. Tightly coil the wire a few times around the base. Snip the excess wire and slide the coil so it tucks into one of the base points.

String 4A or enough beads to fill the space between the 18-gauge base wires at the end of the base. Coil the 26-gauge wire tightly around the opposite base wire 2 times. String enough B to fill the space on the other side of the base and coil the 26-gauge wire tightly around the opposite base wire 2 times. Continue in this manner to embellish the entire base. End by tightly coiling the 26-gauge wire around the base 3 times as you did at the beginning. Trim any excess wire close to the coil. Set aside.

Repeat to create 7 beaded components.

3 **ASSEMBLY.** Cut seven 3½" (8.9cm) pieces of chain; set aside. Open a basic loop at the end of one of the components, attach the end link of one of the chains, and close the loop. Repeat to connect all the components into a circle.

4 **DANGLES.** Cut 2½" (6.6cm) of 26-gauge wire and form a head pin; set aside. Repeat to make a total of 84 head pins. Use a head pin to string 1 crystal. Form a wrapped loop. Repeat to create 42 crystal wrapped-loop dangles. Set aside.

Use a head pin to string 1 pearl. Form a wrapped loop, but before closing, string on a crystal dangle and attach the pearl dangle to one of the chain links. Repeat to add 1 pearl and crystal dangle to each chain link.

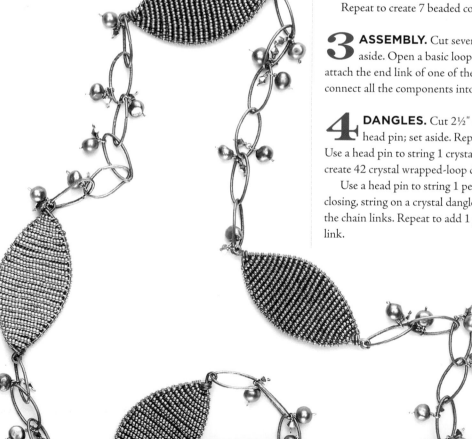

MARQUIS COMPONENT
at-a-glance

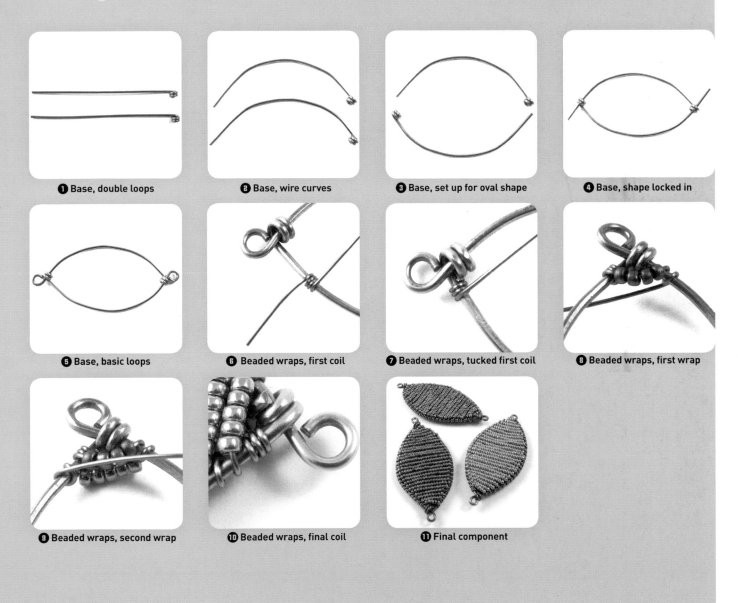

❶ Base, double loops

❷ Base, wire curves

❸ Base, set up for oval shape

❹ Base, shape locked in

❺ Base, basic loops

❻ Beaded wraps, first coil

❼ Beaded wraps, tucked first coil

❽ Beaded wraps, first wrap

❾ Beaded wraps, second wrap

❿ Beaded wraps, final coil

⓫ Final component

Use thick wire to form a sturdy base component and thin wire and beads to embellish it. Make several and combine into a sparkling necklace that's certain to get people talking.

WHAT'S THE STORY?

I once designed a necklace called *Angelina Collier,* named after the film actress Angelina Jolie, whom I envisioned wearing the necklace. The necklace design, which included a huge amount of crystals and sterling silver wire and chain, didn't catch on. My *Shiloh Necklace* is a redesign of Angelina's necklace, this one named after the actress's daughter.

TECHNIQUES
Attaching jump rings
Flush cutting
Head pin
Basic loop
Wrapped loop
Wrapped bead link or dangle
See pages 122–140 for helpful technique information

MATERIALS
120 turquoise 2XAB 3mm crystal bicones (A)
5 g opaque turquoise size 11° seed beads (B)
5 g silver-lined green size 11° seed beads (C)
22 peacock 5–6mm fresh-water potato pearls (D)
20 sterling silver 4mm 20-gauge jump rings
1 sterling silver 6x18mm filigree fishhook clasp
9' (2.7m) of sterling silver 24-gauge dead-soft or half-hard round wire
3' (.9m) of sterling silver 18-gauge dead-soft round wire
22' (6.7m) of sterling silver 26-gauge dead-soft round wire
2' (61cm) of sterling silver 2mm cable chain

TOOLS
Chain-nose pliers
Round-nose pliers
Flush cutters
Wire straighteners
Ruler
3" (7.6cm) piece of scrap 18-gauge wire

FINISHED SIZE
18" (45.7cm)

RACHEL'S TIPS

→ The 18-gauge bases in this necklace don't have to be exactly 3" (7.6cm), but the closer to that measurement they are, the closer the components will match.

→ You can slide the outer embellishment pattern along the 18-gauge base if the embellishment is a little short or squeeze the embellishments together if it's a little long. Just take care to leave the 26-gauge loops intact if moving the embellishment, as they can become so slim and close to the 18-gauge component base that there is no longer a loop.

→ When trimming the excess 26-gauge wire, always cut with the flat side of the cutters toward the work.

→ These components work nicely on a chain as the pendant of a necklace. You can also make two for a pair of earrings.

1 HEAD PINS. Flush cut 2" (7.6cm) of 24-gauge wire and form a head pin; set aside. Repeat to make a total of 46 head pins.

2 BASE. Flush cut a 3" (7.6cm) piece of 18-gauge wire. Use round-nose pliers to form a 3mm basic loop at one wire end. Form another 3mm basic loop at the other wire end in the same direction so the loops form an S shape; continue to roll this loop for an additional 1mm. Use your fingers to bend the wire into a teardrop shape so the smaller loop sits at the top of the shape and the larger loop sits below it, within the teardrop shape.

3 BASE BINDING. Cut 1½' (45.7cm) of 26-gauge wire. Leaving a 1" (2.5cm) tail, tightly coil one wire end around the

base with 2 wraps. Trim the tail wire; slide the coil toward the top of the teardrop shape. Bind the two ends of the base by tightly wrapping the 26-gauge wire around the inner base loop 2 times.

4 BASE EMBELLISHMENT. Use the 26-gauge wire to add beads to the base, then add beaded dangles:

Outer embellishment (left side) String 1A. Hold the bead in position on the outside of the base as you tightly wrap the 26-gauge wire around the base wire 1½ times. Keep the wrap tight against the bead. Repeat to add 1B, 1A, 1B, 1A, 1B, and 1A.

Loop Hold the scrap 18-gauge wire perpendicular to the outer edge of the base. Leave the scrap wire in place as you tightly wrap the 26-gauge wire around the base 1½ times, creating a loop. Remove the scrap wire.

Outer embellishment (right side) Repeat the outer embellishment, left side. Finish the embellishment by wrapping around the inner base loop 2 times.

Inner embellishment String 1C. Wrap the 26-gauge wire between the next two beads. Repeat to add a total of 15C.

Dangles Use a head pin to string 1D; form a wrapped loop that attaches to the inner base loop. Repeat to add another dangle to the loop at the bottom of the base. Set the embellished base aside.

Repeat this entire step to create a total of 11 components.

5 CHAINS. Cut a 6" (15.2cm) piece of chain. Use a jump ring to attach 1 component to the center of the chain. Measure 1" (2.5cm) down the chain and attach another component and another 1" (2.5cm) down the chain; repeat on the other side of the center component. In the same manner, attach 6 components to the center of the remaining 18" (45.7cm) piece of chain.

Lay the short chain so it's centered and parallel to the long chain. Use jump rings to connect the end links of the short chain to the long one.

6 CHAIN DANGLES. Use a head pin to string 1A and form a wrapped loop to create a dangle; set aside. Repeat to make a total of 12 dangles.

Use a head pin to string 1A. Form a wrapped loop but before making the wrap, string a dangle just made and attach to the chain near one of the jump rings that connect the short and long chains. Repeat every 1" (2.5cm) down the chain; repeat on the other side of the necklace.

7 CLASP. Flush cut 3" (7.6cm) of 24-gauge wire. Form a wrapped loop that connects to one half of the clasp. String 1A; form another wrapped loop that connects to one end of the long chain. Repeat to attach the other clasp half to the open end of the long chain.

SHILOH at-a-glance

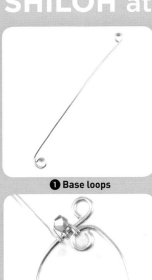

1 Base loops

2 Base teardrop

3 Base binding, beginning coil

4 Base binding

5 Outer base embellishment, first bead

6 Outer base embellishment loop

7 Outer base embellishment end coil

8 Inner base embellishment, first bead

9 Inner base embellishment completed

10 Base embellishment dangles

11 Attaching components to short chain

12 Attaching the short and long chains

13 Chain dangles

14 Beaded link clasp connection

Put your beadworking skills to task as you create these beautiful beaded beads. They look great alone on a simple chain, or incorporate them with other beads for an elaborate design.

WHAT'S THE STORY?

This project was designed shortly after *Ootheca Cuff,* page 8. Having made several of the cuffs with a regimented 4-bead right-angle weave, I was ready for something completely different, and out came the *Oothecal Bedes,* named for their similarity to *Ootheca Cuff,* but different enough to stand on their own.

TECHNIQUES
Right-angle weave
Tubular peyote stitch
See pages 122–140 for helpful technique information.

MATERIALS
LARGE BEDE
5 g dark pink matte size
    11° seed beads (A)
1 g green iris size
    11° seed beads (B)
1 g silver-lined ruby AB size
    11° seed beads (C)
1 g opaque pea AB size
    11° seed beads (D)
1 g green iris size
    8° seed beads (E)
24 jet 2XAB 3mm crystal
    bicones
Gray or smoke beading thread

SMALL BEDE
2 g dark pink matte size
11° seed beads (A)
1 g green iris size
    11° seed beads (B)
1 g silver-lined ruby AB size
    11° seed beads (C)
1 g opaque pea AB size
    11° seed beads (D)
1 g green iris size
    8° seed beads (E)
6 jet 2XAB 3mm crystal
    bicones
Gray or smoke beading thread

TOOLS
Size 12 beading needles
Thread snips or small scissors

FINISHED SIZE
Small Bead 30x12m
Large Bead 32x22mm

Large Bede

1 BASE. Use a comfortable length of thread and A to right-angle weave a base as in FIGURE 1.

Row 1, Unit 1 String 15A; tie a square knot to form a tight circle, leaving a 6" (15.2cm) tail. Pass through the first 4A.

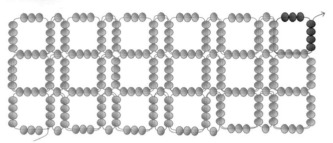

FIGURE 1

Row 1, Unit 2 String 6A; pass through the 4A last exited from the previous unit and the first 5A just added.

Row 1, Unit 3 String 11A; pass through the 4A last exited from the previous unit and the first 8A just added.

Row 1, Units 4–11 Repeat Row 1 Units 2 and 3 to form a row 6 units long. Exit from the top 4A of the last unit.

Row 2, Unit 1 String 12A; pass through the top 4A of the last Row 1 unit, the 12A just added, and the top 1A of the next Row 1 unit.

Row 2, Unit 2 String 5A; pass through the side 4A of the previous Row 2 unit, the top 1A of the next Row 1 unit, and the first 4A just added.

Row 2, Unit 3 String 8A; pass through the top 4A of the next Row 1 unit, the side 4A of the previous Row 2 unit, the 8A just added, and the top 1A of the next Row 1 unit.

Row 2, Units 4–11 Repeat Row 2 Units 2 and 3 to the end of the row. Exit from the top 4A of the last unit.

Row 3, Unit 1 String 11A; pass through the top 4A of the last Row 2 unit, the 11A just added, and the top 1A of the next Row 2 unit.

Row 3, Unit 2 String 5A; pass through the side 4A of the previous Row 3 unit, the top 1A of the next Row 2 unit, and the first 4A just added.

Row 3, Unit 3 String 7A; pass through the top 4A of the next Row 2 unit, the side 4A of the previous Row 3 unit, the 7A just added, and the top 1A of the next Row 2 unit.

Row 3, Units 4–11 Repeat Row 3 Units 2 and 3 to the end of the

row. Exit up through 4A on the outside of the last unit.

2 ZIPPED EDGES. Bring the base ends together (FIGURE 2). String 1A and pass up through the side 4A at the other end of Row 3; string 1A and pass down through the side 4A of the last Row 3 unit, the first 1A just added, and up through the side 4A of the other end of Row 2, through 1A just added, and up through 4A of the adjacent Row 2 unit. String 1A and pass down through the side 4A on the other end of Row 2; weave through the beads to exit from the 1A just added and up through the side 4A of the adjacent Row 1 unit. String 1A and pass down through the side 4A of the other end of Row 1, the adjacent 1A (FIGURE 3), and up through the side 3A of the adjacent Row 1 unit to complete the base tube (FIGURE 4).

3 SMALL BUMP. Work tubular peyote stitch off of a large unit in the base tube's Row 1:

Round 1 String 1A; pass through the middle 1A of the next 3A side in the same unit (FIGURE 5). String 1A and pass through the 2A of the next 4A side; repeat 2 times. Step up for this and subsequent rounds by passing through the first bead added in the round (FIGURE 6).

Round 2 String 1A and pass through the next 1A from Round 1. String 2A and pass through the next 1A from Round 1; repeat 2 times (FIGURE 7).

FIGURE 2

FIGURE 3

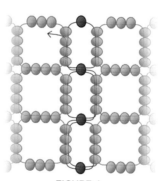

FIGURE 4

FIGURE 5

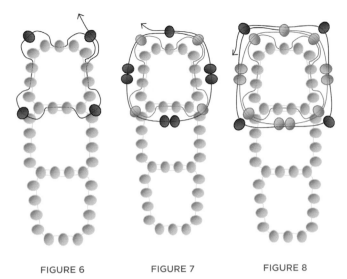

| FIGURE 6 | FIGURE 7 | FIGURE 8 | FIGURE 9 |

Round 3 String 1A and pass through the next 2A from Round 2; repeat 2 times. String 1A and pass through the next 1A from Round 2 (FIGURE 8)

Round 4 String 1B and pass through the next 1A from Round 3; repeat 3 times. Pass through the first 1B added in this round (FIGURE 9). Pass through the next 1A from Round 3 and pass through the 4B added in this round 2 times to close the bump (FIGURE 10).

Repeat to add a small bump to each of the 6 large units in Base Row 1.

RACHEL'S TIPS

→ These beads look great strung together as the focal point of a necklace. In the necklace shown, I used 14x8mm lampworked rondelles made by Lea Zinke to space the beads apart from each other, then strung the strap using 6x4mm fire-polished rondelles and 3mm crystal bicones.

→ When working the bumps, pass through the four beads of the last rounds two times for extra security. That goes for the crystals, too—you want your beadwork to be *fuerte!*

4 **LARGE BUMP.** Weave through beads to exit from the middle 2A at the top of the adjacent Row 2 base unit. Embellish the unit with tubular peyote stitch:

Round 1 String 1A and pass through the middle 2A of the next side in same unit; repeat to add a total of 4A. Step up through the first 1A added in this round (FIGURE 11).

Round 2 String 2C and pass through the next 1A from the previous round; repeat to add a total

FIGURE 10

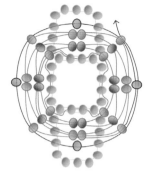

FIGURE 15

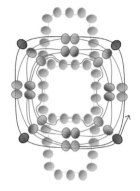

FIGURE 16

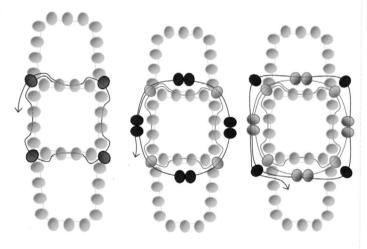

FIGURE 11   FIGURE 12   FIGURE 13

of 8C. Step up through the first 2C added in this round (FIGURE 12).

Round 3 String 1C and pass through the next 2C from the previous round; repeat to add a total of 4C. Step up through the first 1C added in this round (FIGURE 13).

Round 4 Repeat Round 2 using 2B in each stitch (FIGURE 14).

Round 5 Repeat Round 3 using 1B in each stitch (FIGURE 15).

Round 6 String 1D and pass through next 1B from the previous round; repeat to add a total of 4D (FIGURE 16). Pass through the 4D added in this round 2 times to close the bump.

Repeat to add a large bump to each of the 6 large units in Base Row 2.

Weave through beads to exit the middle 2A at the top of Base Row 3. Repeat the small bump sequence to embellish each of the 6 large units in Base Row 3.

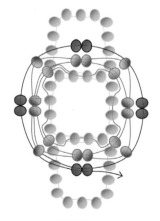

FIGURE 14

FIGURE 17

5 **CRYSTALS.** Weave through the base beads to exit down through the first, second, and third A on the side of a Base Row 1 unit. String 1 bicone and pass down through the middle 2A in the adjacent Base Row 2 unit. String 1 bicone and pass down through the second, third, and fourth A on the side of the adjacent Base Row 3 unit. Pass back through the beads, repeating the thread path to reinforce. Repeat to add 2 bicones down the sides of each set of small base units (FIGURE 17).

FIGURE 18

6 **END.** Weave through beads to exit 1A at the top of a small unit from Base Row 3. Work circular peyote stitch off this right-angle weave row to close the bead's end:

Round 1 String 1A, skip 1A, and pass through the following 1A. Repeat to work 1A in each stitch, adding a total of 18A (FIGURE 18). Step up for this and all subsequent rounds by passing through the first bead added in the round.

Round 2 Alternate working 1 decrease with 1A to add a total of 9A (FIGURE 19).

Round 3 Work 1E in each stitch to add a total of 9E (FIGURE 20).

Round 4 String 1A, pass through 2E from Round 3. String 1A, pass through 1E from Round 3. Repeat to add a total of 6A (FIGURE 21).

Round 5 Work 1A in each stitch to add a total of 6A (FIGURE 22). Pass through the 6A two more times to close the end.

Picots Weave through beads to exit 1A in Round 2. String 1A, 1C, and 1A and pass through the next 1A from Round 2 ; repeat to add a total of 9 picots.

Weave through the beadwork to the other side of the beaded bead. Repeat this step to close the other end. Secure the thread and trim.

FIGURE 19

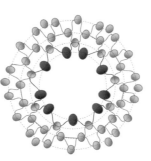

FIGURE 20

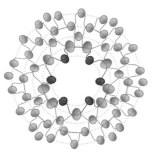

FIGURE 21

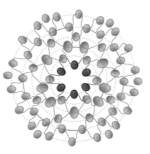

FIGURE 22

**Oothecal Bedes—
"Turquoise" variation**

LARGE BEDE
at-a-glance

1 Base

2 Folding base in half

3 Zipped edges

4 Small bump, Round 1, first stitch

5 Small bump, Round 1 step up

6 Small bump, Round 2 step up

7 Small bump, Round 3 step up

8 Small bump, Round 4 step up

9 End, Round 1, first stitch

10 End, Round 1 step up

11 End, Round 2, making a decrease

12 End, Round 2 step up

⓭ End, Round 3 step up

⓮ End, Round 4 step up

⓯ End, Round 5 step up.

⓰ End, Round 5 closing end

⓱ End, Picot, first stitch

⓲ End Picots

**Oothecal Bedes—
"Topace" Variation**

OOTHECAL BEDES

Small Bede

1 BASE. Use a comfortable length of thread and A to right-angle weave a base as in (FIGURE 1).

Unit 1 String 12A and tie a square knot to form a tight circle, leaving a 6" (15.2cm) tail. Pass through the first 3A strung.

FIGURE 1

Unit 2 String 5A; pass through the 3A last exited from the previous unit and the first 4A just added.

Unit 3 String 9A; pass through the side 3A of the previous unit and the first 6A just added.

Units 4–11 Repeat Units 2 and 3 until there are 6 large units.

Ring Fold the base in half so the ends touch. String 1A and pass up through the side 3A of the first unit. String 1A and pass down through the side 3A of sixth unit. Pass through the first 1A added in this step and the first 2A of the adjacent side (FIGURE 2).

FIGURE 2

2 BUMP. Work tubular peyote stitch to embellish a large base unit:

Round 1 String 1A and pass through the middle 1A of the next side in the same unit; repeat 3 times for a total of 4A. Step up through the first 1A added in this round (FIGURE 3).

Round 2 String 1C and pass through the next 1A from Round 1; repeat 3 times for a total of 4C. Step up through the first 1C

FIGURE 3

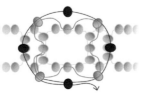

FIGURE 4

added in this round (FIGURE 4).

Rounds 3 and 4 Repeat Round 2 two times using 1B in each stitch (FIGURE 5).

Round 5 String 1D and pass through the next 1B from Round 4; repeat 3 times for a total of 4D (FIGURE 6). Pass through the first 1D in this round, the next 1B from Round 4, and the following 1D of this round. Pass through the 4D added in this round 2 times to close the bump.

FIGURE 5

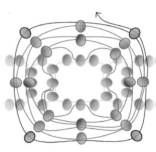

FIGURE 6

3 CRYSTAL. Weave through beads to exit down through 3A on the side of a small base unit. String 1 bicone and pass down through 3A of opposite side of the same unit. Pass through the bottom 1A of the unit, through the bicone, and down through the side 2A to set up for the next bump (FIGURE 7).

Alternate the Bump and Crystal embellishments along the base.

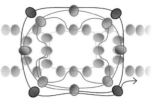

FIGURE 7

4 ENDS. Repeat Step 6 for the Large Bede to complete the ends of the small beaded bead.

SMALL BEDE
at-a-glance

1 Base

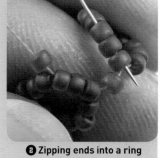

2 Zipping ends into a ring

3 Bump, Round 1 step up

4 Bump, Round 2 step up

5 Bump, Round 3 step up

6 Bump, Round 4 step up

7 Bump, Round 5 step up

8 Crystal, first stitch

9 Crystal, second stitch

10 Crystal, final stitch

Seed-bead fronds extend from a beaded base, resembling points of the archetypal jester's hat in this lively herringbone-stitched bracelet design.

WHAT'S THE STORY?

In the Middle Ages, jester hats were distinctive. Made of cloth, they were floppy with three points called "liliripes." With humorous effect, the points represented the ass's ears and tail. In this project title, "H" is for the herringbone stitch employed for the base.

TECHNIQUES
Stop bead
Ladder stitch
Herringbone stitch
See pages 122–140 for helpful technique information.

MATERIALS
11 g each of size 8° seed beads in opaque red (A8), silver-lined light sapphire (B8), opaque orange (C8), silver-lined berry (D8), purple luster (E8), and cream-lined olive AB (F8)
2 g each of size 11° seed beads in opaque red (A11), silver-lined teal (B11), transparent orange AB (C11), silver-lined berry (D11), lavender-lined sapphire (E11), and silver-lined sage (F11)
0.5 g each of size 15° seed beads purple luster (A15), silver-lined teal (B15), opaque orange (C15), silver-lined fuchsia (D15), opaque lavender (E15), and spring green luster (F15)
31 each of 3.4mm Japanese fringe drops in green-lined green, indigo matte, pink-lined clear, orange-lined orange, pink-lined blue, and red
2 sapphire AB 14mm glass buttons with shank
1½' (45.7cm) elastic floss
Gray or smoke beading thread

TOOLS
Size 12 beading needles
1 wide-eye needle
Thread snips or small scissors

FINISHED SIZE
7" (17.8cm)

1 BASE.
Use size 8° beads to form the bracelet's base:

Row 1 Tie a stop bead onto the end of a comfortable length of working thread. Form a strip of ladder stitch 12 beads long in this order: 2A8, 2B8, 2C8, 2D8, 2E8, and 2F8 (FIGURE 1).

FIGURE 1

Row 2 Remove the stop bead. Working with the same color size 8° you last exited, work herringbone stitch, 2 size 8's in each stitch (FIGURE 2), across the row. Make a turnaround by tying a half-hitch knot around the thread between the adjacent 2A8 from the previous row. Step up to the next and subsequent rows by passing up through the 2 edge beads (FIGURE 3).

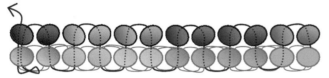

FIGURE 2

FIGURE 3

Row 3 Repeat Row 2, this time making the turnaround by tying a half-hitch knot around the thread between the adjacent 2F8 from the previous row (FIGURE 4).

Rows 4–63 Repeat Rows 2 and 3 until the base is 63 rows long or your desired length. Bind the last row's beads by working a ladder-stitch thread path with no beads added. Secure the thread and trim.

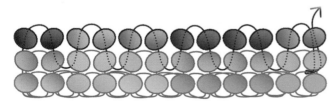

FIGURE 4

2 FRINGE.
Start a new thread that exits from 1A8 in the base's second-to-last row, toward the beadwork. Work one 2-bead-high ladder-stitched fringe up from every other set of two base beads, as indicated by the orange arrows in FIGURE 5:

Fringe 1 String 2A8 and pass through the adjacent 1A8 on the base. Pass back through the second

FIGURE 6

FIGURE 7

FIGURE 8

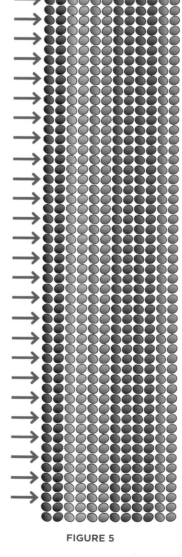

FIGURE 5

FIGURE 9

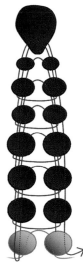

FIGURE 10

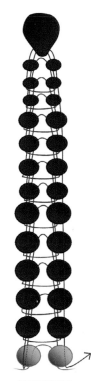

FIGURE 11

1A8 just added, down through the first 1A8 added, and through 1A8 of the base. This will center the fringe (FIGURES 6, 7 AND 8). Pass back through the first 1A8 added in this step.

Work 2-bead-high ladder stitch off the 2A8 just placed in this order: 2A8 four times; 2A11 three times; and 2A15 two times. String 1 red drop, reinforce with a second pass through the drop bead, and pass down through the opposite herringbone-stitched base column. Weave through beads to exit from 1A8 two rows down the base (FIGURE 9). **Note:** When you work the ladder-stitch fringe, weave down through 2 rows instead of the usual 1; this will give the fringe added strength.

Fringe 2 Repeat Fringe 1, this time stitching 2A8 three times, 2A11 two times, 2A15 once, and 1 red drop (FIGURE 10).

Fringe 3 Repeat Fringe 1, this time stitching 2A8 two times, 2A11 once, 2A15 once, and 1 red drop (FIGURE 11).

Fringe 4 Repeat Fringe 1, this time stitching 2A8 once, 2A11 once, 2A15 once, and 1 red drop (FIGURE 12).

Fringes 5-7 Repeat Fringes 1–3 in reverse for a total of 3 fringes.

Fringe 8 Repeat Fringe 1, this time stitching 2A8 five times, 2A11 four times, 2A15 three times, and 1 red drop (FIGURE 13).

Fringes 9-end Repeat Fringes 1–8 until you have added a fringe to every other row. The fringe lengths should undulate.

Repeat this step down each column on the herringbone base, using the appropriately colored beads, until the entire base is embellished.

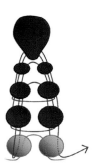

FIGURE 12

3 CLASP. Add a button and loop closure to the end of the base:

Buttons Weave through beads to exit out from 1B8 at one end of the base. String 1 button and pass through the base's adjacent 1B8, exiting out toward the base end. Pass back through button and through the original 1B8 you exited, out toward the end. Repeat the thread path to reinforce. Weave through beads of the row to exit 1E8 and add the second button in the same manner. Secure the thread and trim.

Loops Thread the wide-eye needle with the elastic and slide the needle to the center of the elastic to work doubled. Secure the elastic to the other end of the base and exit from 1B8. String 11B8, or enough B8 to fit snugly around the button on the mirror end of the bracelet. Pass back through the adjacent 1B8 on the base end and pull up the slack. Weave through beads to add another loop to the E8 beads on the base end. Secure the elastic and trim.

FIGURE 13

RACHEL'S TIPS

→ If you choose six different colored stripes, that can add up to a lot of beads on the ol' workbench at one time. To simplify things, work one colored stripe at a time.

→ My favorite place to finish and add thread is on the fringe. Work it as though it were the edge of flat herringbone.

→ Before adding the clasp loops, make sure the elastic floss is not slipping through the beadwork at all.

H. LILIRIPES at-a-glance

1 Base, Row 1, first ladder stitch

2 Base, Row 1

5 Base, Row 2 turnaround knot

3 Base, Row 2, first herringbone stitch

4 Base, Row 2

6 Base, Row 2 step up

7 Base, Row 3 turnaround knot

8 Base, Row 3 step up

9 Base, end-row ladder stitch

10 Fringe 1, first stitch

11 Fringe 1, centering the first stitch (a)

12 Fringe 1, centering the first stitch (b)

13 Fringe 1, centering the first stitch (c)

14 Fringe 1, step up for second stitch

15 Fringe 1

16 Clasp, centering the button (a)

17 Clasp, centering the button (b)

18 Clasp, centering the button (c)

19 Clasp, adding the loop (a)

20 Clasp, adding the loop (b)

21 Clasp loop

The beadwork in this sculpted right-angle-weave and tubular-peyote-stitch component bursts like a supernova around a super twinkling crystal rivoli.

WHAT'S THE STORY?

I wondered how a round right-angle-weave base would turn out. After a bit of experimenting, a flat ring of beads emerged tailored to accommodate a five-sided *Ootheca Cuff* bump. The embellished ring was interesting, but the large hole in the middle was a problem, so I dug through my drawer of beading starts and mis-starts for inspiration. In the bead wreckage, I found a peyote-bezeled rivoli that was the perfect match, size- and color-wise, to fill the hole. A little zipping up and the component was complete.

TECHNIQUES
Right-angle weave
Tubular peyote stitch
Head pin
Wrapped loop
Crimping
See pages 122–140 for helpful technique information.

MATERIALS
2 g aqua-lined aqua translucent matte size 11° seed beads (A)
1 g silver-lined aqua size 11° seed beads (B)
1 g white-lined gray AB size 11° seed beads (C)
1 g gold iris matte size 15° seed beads (D)
1 g 22k gold metallic size 15° seed beads (E)
9 gold-lined aqua 3.4mm glass drops (F)
18 dark green iris 3.4mm glass drops (G)
1 olivine 14mm crystal rivoli
77 aqua 5mm freshwater potato pearls
4 olivine 3mm crystal rounds
4 gold 1x1mm crimp tubes
1 gold 10x22mm foldover or box clasp
Gray or smoke beading thread
24" (61cm) of fine flexible beading wire
2" (5.1cm) of gold 24-gauge round wire

TOOLS
Size 12 beading needles
Thread snips or small scissors
Chain-nose pliers
Crimping pliers
Round-nose pliers
Wire cutters

FINISHED SIZE
20" (51cm)

1 BASE.
BASE. Use single thread to create a circular right-angle weave as shown in FIGURE 1.

Unit 1 String 16A and tie a square knot to form a circle, leaving a 6" (15.2cm) tail. Pass through the first 4A added.

Unit 2 String 10A; pass through the 4A last exited and the first 5A just added.

Unit 3 String 12A; pass through the 4A last exited from the previous unit and the first 9A just added.

Units 4–11 Repeat Units 2 and 3 to form 6 large units and 5 small ones.

Unit 12 String 1A and pass through the side 4A of Unit 1. String 5A and pass through the side 4A of Unit 11.

FIGURE 1   FIGURE 2

2 BUMP.
BUMP. Weave through beads to exit from the middle 1A of the 3-bead side of a large base unit. Work tubular peyote stitch off the base unit:

Round 1 String 1B and pass through the middle 2A on the next side of the base (FIGURE 2). String 1B and pass through the second 1A of the 5-bead side. String 1B and pass through the fourth 1B of the 5-bead side. String 1B and pass through the middle 2A of the next side. String 1B and pass through middle 1A of the 3-bead side (FIGURE 3). Step up for the next and subsequent rounds by passing through the first bead added in this round.

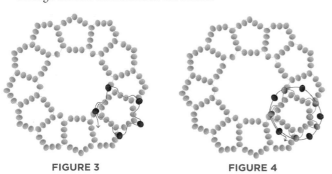

FIGURE 3   FIGURE 4

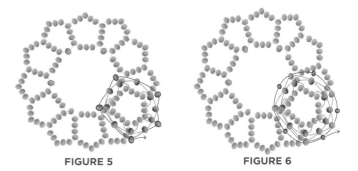

FIGURE 5   FIGURE 6

Round 2 String 1B and pass through the next 1B from Round 1; repeat 4 times to add a total of 5B (FIGURE 4).

Round 3 Repeat Round 2 using 1C in each stitch (FIGURE 5).

Round 4 Repeat Round 2 using 1D in each stitch (FIGURE 6).

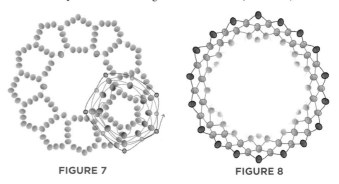

FIGURE 7   FIGURE 8

Round 5 Repeat Round 2 using 1E in each stitch (FIGURE 7). Pass through the next 1D of Round 4. Pass through all 5E of this round 2 times to close the bump.

Repeat this step to embellish all 6 large base units with bumps.

3 RISER.
RISER. Weave through beads to exit from the first 1A of the 3-bead side of a large base unit. Work 3 rounds of tubular peyote stitch off the center ring of the base:

Round 1 String 1A, skip 1A on the base, and pass through the next 1A; repeat to add a total of 18A. Step up for this and subsequent rounds by passing through the first bead added in this round.

Round 2 String 1A and pass through the next 1A from the previous round; repeat to add a total of 18A.

Round 3 Repeat Round 2 (FIGURE 8). Secure the thread and trim; set aside.

FIGURE 9

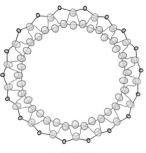

FIGURE 10

4 **BEZEL.** Begin with single thread to work a tubular-peyote-stitch bezel for the rivoli:

Rounds 1 and 2 String 36C and tie a square knot to form a circle, leaving a 6" (15.2cm) tail. Pass through the first 1C added.

Round 3 String 1C, skip 1C from the previous round, and pass through the next 1C; repeat to add a total of 18C (FIGURE 9). Step up for this and subsequent rounds by passing through the first bead added in this round.

Round 4 Work tubular peyote stitch with 1D in each stitch for a total of 18D (FIGURE 10).

Round 5 Repeat Round 4 using 1E in each stitch (FIGURE 11).

Round 6 String 1E and pass through the next 2E of the previous round; repeat to add a total of 9E (FIGURE 12).

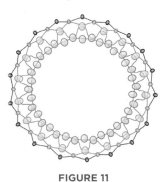

FIGURE 11

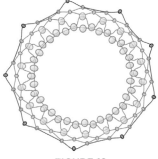

FIGURE 12

RACHEL'S TIPS

→ Make one *O. Bersten Component* to use as a stunning focal piece, make five connected with 6mm jump rings for a bracelet, or make thirty-four and connect them with 6mm jump rings to create an over-the-top necklace, such as Sparkle-Fest assistant Liz Penn and I did (above).

→ Make sure to reinforce the six open right-angle-weave sections, particularly if you're planning to connect them with jump rings. The tighter, stronger connection will ensure your jewelry stays intact.

→ Transitioning from the right-angle-weave large base into the peyote-stitched riser can sometimes be troublesome. Set aside 18A before starting the riser to help keep track of how many beads you need to add.

Round 7 Weave through beads to exit 1C in Round 1. Repeat Round 4.

Round 8 Repeat Round 5. When you have completed half of the round, place the rivoli, face side up, in the center of the beadwork; finish the round.

Round 9 Repeat Round 6, pulling the thread tightly to bezel the rivoli in place (FIGURE 13).

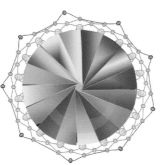

FIGURE 13

Double the thread by pulling the tail past the point where the working thread exits the beadwork. Pass through several beads on the bezel.

5 BEZEL EMBELLISHMENT.

Work rounds of embellishment off the bezel rounds:

Round 1 Weave through beads to exit 1C in Bezel Round 1. String 1F and pass through the next 1C in the round, then string 1E and pass through the next 1C in the round; repeat to add a total of 9E and 9F (FIGURE 14). Step down to exit from 1C in Bezel Round 2.

FIGURE 14

Round 2 String 1G and pass through the next 1C; repeat around to add a total of 18G (FIGURE 15).

6 ZIP COMPONENTS.
Connect the riser and the bezel by peyote stitching the beads of Bezel Round 3 and Riser Round 3 together.
Note: No beads are being added, you're just joining the 2 pieces.
Secure the thread and trim. Set the component aside.

FIGURE 15

7 SPACERS. Use 8" (20.3cm) of thread to string 6E. Tie a square knot to form a tight circle and pass through the beads again (FIGURE 16). Tie an overhand knot between beads and pass through the following bead; repeat around the circle (FIGURE 17). Secure the thread and trim. Set aside. Repeat to make 12 spacers.

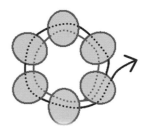

FIGURE 16

8 DROP. Use chain-nose pliers to form a head pin with the 24-gauge wire. String 1 pearl and form a wrapped loop that attaches to an open unit at the bottom of the component.

9 ASSEMBLY. Cut 1' (30.5cm) of beading wire. String 1 crimp tube and 12E, leaving a 1" (2.5cm) tail. Pass

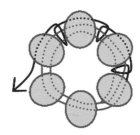

FIGURE 17

through the upper right open unit of the component and back through the tube; crimp the tube. String 1 crystal round, 1 spacer, 3 pearls, 1 spacer, 1 crystal round, 1 spacer, 32 pearls, 1 spacer, 1 crystal round, 1 spacer, 3 pearls, 1 spacer, 1 crystal round, 1 crimp tube, and one half of the clasp. Pass back through the crimp tube, snug the beads, and crimp the tube. Trim any excess wire. Repeat this step to finish the other side of the necklace.

O. BERSTEN COMPONENT
at-a-glance

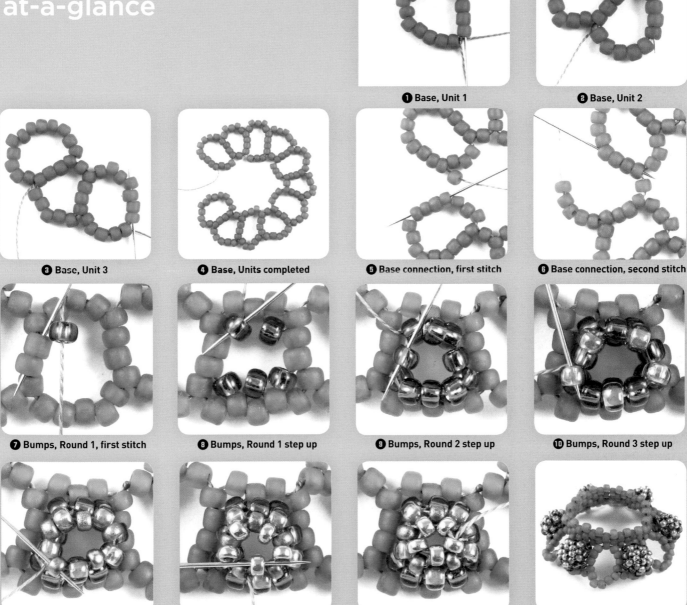

❶ Base, Unit 1

❷ Base, Unit 2

❸ Base, Unit 3

❹ Base, Units completed

❺ Base connection, first stitch

❻ Base connection, second stitch

❼ Bumps, Round 1, first stitch

❽ Bumps, Round 1 step up

❾ Bumps, Round 2 step up

❿ Bumps, Round 3 step up

⓫ Bumps, Round 4 step up

⓬ Bumps, Round 5 step up

⓭ Bump, closed

⓮ Riser

⑮ Bezel, Rounds 1 and 2

⑯ Bezel, Round 3, first stitch

⑰ Bezel, Round 4, first stitch

⑱ Bezel, Round 5, first stitch

⑲ Bezel, Round 5 step up

⑳ Bezel, Round 6 decrease

㉑ Bezel, Round 7, first stitch

㉒ Bezel, Round 8, first stitch

㉓ Bezel, Round 8, placing rivoli

㉔ Bezeled rivoli

㉕ Bezel embellishment, Round 1, second stitch

㉖ Bezel embellishment, Round 2, first stitch

㉗ Zipping riser and bezel

㉘ Spacer

O. Bersten Component—
"Chocolate" (left), "Pink and Green" (middle),
and "Aqua Gold" (right) variations

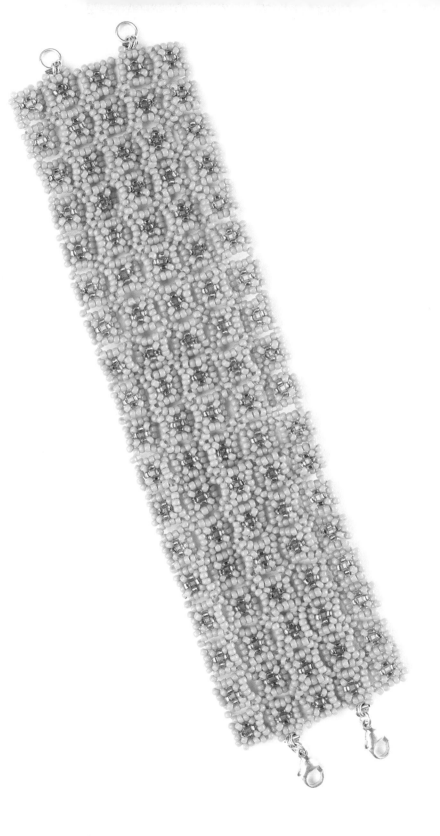

This versatile right-angle-weave and tubular-peyote-stitch cuff resembles a flying carpet mosaic, full of magical possibilities.

WHAT'S THE STORY?

The *Ootheca Cuff* (page 8) was a much-discussed project in beadweaving classes. After hearing similar comments from different beaders, I decided to design a cuff with more immediate gratification and a lower price tag while maintaining some of the charming attributes of the *Ootheca Cuff.* As the first two pieces were worked up simultaneously, limitless shapes and colorways danced before my eyes. I've included several of the patterns here, plus a blank template for you to make your mark, too.

TECHNIQUES
Attaching jump rings
Right-angle weave
Tubular peyote stitch
See pages 122–140 for helpful technique information.

MATERIALS
22 g size 11° seed beads (see Patterns on page 96 for colorways)
2 sterling silver 1x4mm tubes
2 sterling silver 7x11mm lobster clasps
8–12 sterling silver 4mm 18- to 20-gauge jump rings
2 sterling silver 7mm split rings (for use with lobster clasp)
Gray or smoke beading thread

TOOLS
Size 12 beading needles
2 pairs of chain-nose pliers
Thread snips or small scissors

FINISHED SIZE
7½" (19.1cm)

RACHEL'S TIPS

→ This bracelet works up fairly quickly, so try out more than one of the patterns to test your mental flexibility.

→ If you aren't sure how long you'd like your bracelet to be, make the base one or two units shorter. You can add more rows later.

→ Make the cuff narrower or wider by adding or reducing the base rows.

→ A 32mm sliding lock clasp with two or more loops works well as a clasp for this bracelet. Simply use 4mm jump rings to attach the clasp loops to the silver tubes. If you have a five-loop slide clasp, first add silver tubes to the ends of base Row 3, then flush cut the second and fourth loops on the clasp for a perfect match.

1 BASE. Following one of the base patterns on page 96 for bead color placement, use a single length of thread to stitch a right-angle-weave base:

Row 1, Unit 1 String 16 beads and tie a square knot to form a tight circle, leaving a 6" (15.2cm) tail. Pass through the first 4 beads just strung (FIGURE 1).

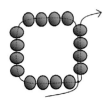

FIGURE 1

Row 1, Unit 2 String 6 beads, pass through the last 4 beads exited from the previous unit and the first 5 beads just added (FIGURE 2).

FIGURE 2

Row 1, Unit 3 String 12 beads, pass through the last 4 beads exited from the previous unit, and the first 8 beads just added (FIGURE 3).

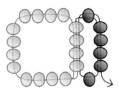

FIGURE 3

Row 1, Units 4 and on Repeat Units 2 and 3 for a total of 9 units wide.

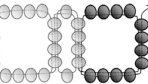

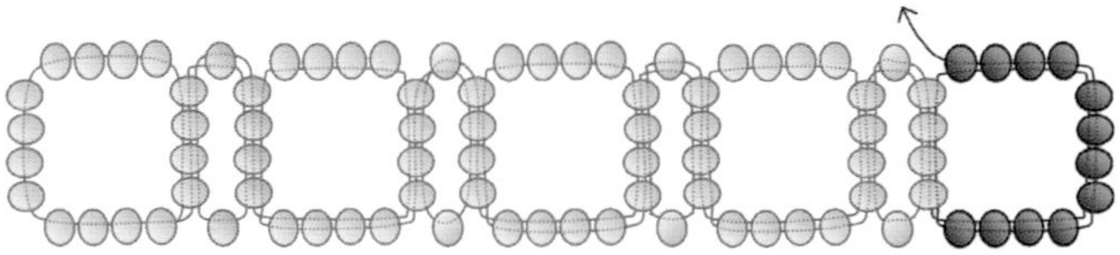

FIGURE 4

Exit from the top 4A of the last unit (FIGURE 4). Make sure the last unit duplicates Unit 3 (a 16-bead unit).

Row 2, Unit 1 String 6 beads, pass through the 4 beads last exited from the previous unit, and the first bead just added (FIGURE 5).

Row 2, Unit 2 String 2 beads, pass through the top bead of the adjacent unit from the previous row, the side bead of the previous Row 2 unit, the 2 beads just added, and through the 4 top beads of the following unit from the previous row (FIGURE 6).

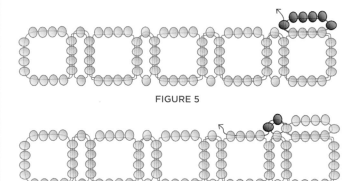

FIGURE 5

FIGURE 6

Row 2, Unit 3 String 5 beads, pass through the side beads of the adjacent unit from the previous Row 2 unit, the 4 beads last exited from the previous row, and the first bead just added (FIGURE 7).

Row 2, Units 4 and on Repeat Row 2, Units 2 and 3 to the end of the row. Exit from the top 4A of the last unit (FIGURE 8).

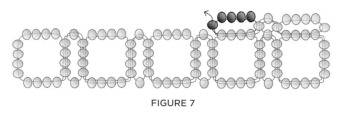

FIGURE 7

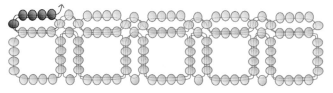

FIGURE 8

Row 3, Unit 1 String 12 beads, pass through the 4 beads last exited, and the first 4 beads just added (FIGURE 9).

Row 3, Unit 2 String 5 beads, pass through the top bead of the adjacent unit in the previous row, the 4 beads last exited from the previous Row 3 unit, the 5 beads just added, and the 4 top beads of the following unit from the previous row (FIGURE 10).

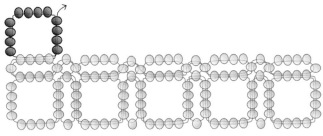

FIGURE 9

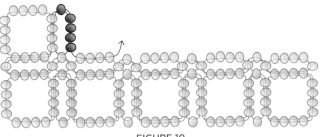

FIGURE 10

Row 3, Unit 3 String 8 beads, pass through the side beads of the adjacent unit from the previous Row 3 unit, the 4 side beads of the adjacent unit in the previous row, and the first 4 beads just added (FIGURE 11).

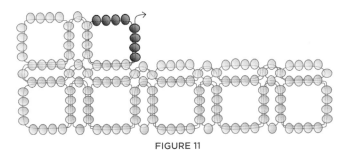

FIGURE 11

Row 3, Units 4 and on Repeat Row 3 units 2 and 3 to the end of the row. Exit from the top 4A of the last unit (FIGURE 12).

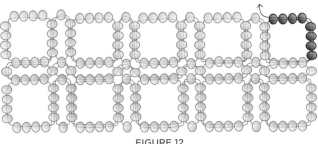

FIGURE 12

Rows 4–18 Repeat Rows 2 and 3 to make a base 18 large units long.

2 FILL. Following the same color pattern for bead color placement, use single thread to fill each 16-bead base unit with tubular peyote stitch:

Round 1 Weave through the base beads to exit from the third bead on any side of a 16-bead unit. String 1 bead and pass through the middle 2 beads of the next side in the same unit; repeat to add a total of 4 beads (FIGURE 13). Step up through the first bead added in this round.

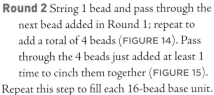

FIGURE 13

Round 2 String 1 bead and pass through the next bead added in Round 1; repeat to add a total of 4 beads (FIGURE 14). Pass through the 4 beads just added at least 1 time to cinch them together (FIGURE 15). Repeat this step to fill each 16-bead base unit.

FIGURE 14

3 ENDS. Weave through the beadwork to exit from the first bead of an end Column 2 base unit. String 1 size 11°, 1 silver tube, and 1 size 11°; skip over 2 base beads in the same Column 2 unit and pass through the fourth bead. Pull up the slack. Weave through the connection several times to reinforce. Repeat this step at the end of Column 4. Secure the thread and trim. Repeat this entire step at the other end of the bracelet.

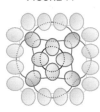

FIGURE 15

4 CLASP. Use two 4mm jump rings to attach 1 lobster clasp to 1 silver tube. Repeat to add the second clasp to the same end. Use the same method to attach the 7mm split rings to the tubes at the other end of the bracelet.

PATTERNS

Each pattern is displayed with two colors of thread path.
The red thread path indicates the BASE as in the directions
on page 94. The blue thread path indicates the FILL as in
the directions on page 95.

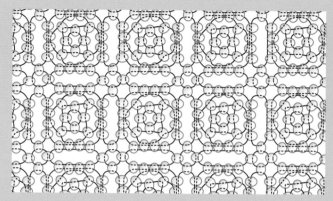

BLANK

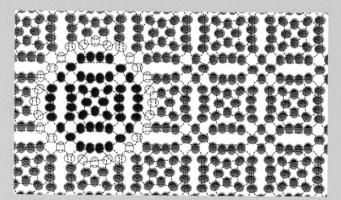

BALANCE

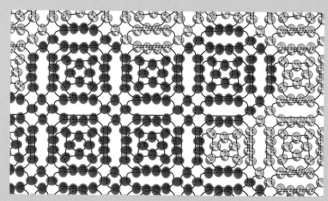

BRINJAL

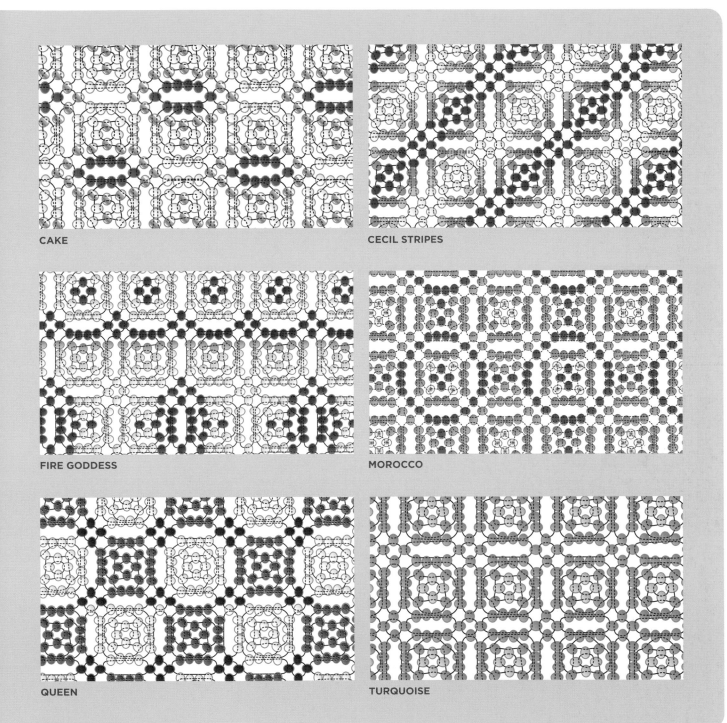

CAKE

CECIL STRIPES

FIRE GODDESS

MOROCCO

QUEEN

TURQUOISE

O. MOSAIC CUFF
at-a-glance

1 End, beginning point

2 End, attaching loop

3 Ends

4 Clasps

5 Clasp rings

6 Sliding clasp variation

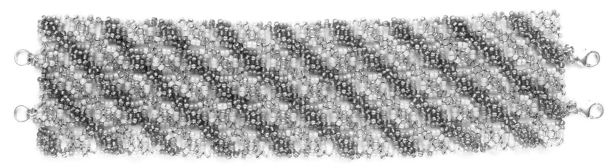

CECIL STRIPES VARIATION

TURQUOISE VARIATION

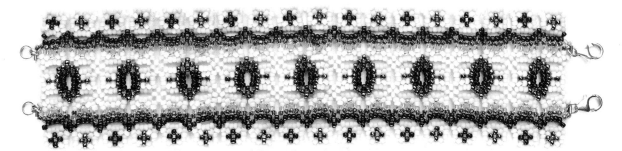

FIRE GODDESS VARIATION

VARIATION

Create this bangle by joining dimensional right-angle weave and tubular peyote stitch in radial symmetry, conjuring up one of the most recognized and loved sea creatures.

WHAT'S THE STORY?

The muse who inspired this project is bright, sprightly New Yorker Suzanne Golden, a talented beader in her own right. Clad in edgy and daringly shaped and colored clothing and jewelry, she exemplifies the excitement and beauty to be found in fashion extremes. The orange version was the first *Sea Star Bangle* because orange was the color on the bead bench that day. As the first ray grew taller and taller, Suzanne's influence on my work was apparent.

TECHNIQUES
Right-angle weave
Tubular even-count peyote
    stitch
*See pages 122–140 for helpful
    technique information.*

MATERIALS
25 g matte blue AB size
    11° seed beads (A)
15 g metallic peacock
    11° seed beads (B)
4 g metallic silver size
    11° seed beads (C)
10 g opaque white size
    11° seed beads (D)
Gray or smoke beading thread
Beeswax (optional)

TOOLS
Size 12 beading needle
Thread snips or small scissors

FINISHED SIZE
7½" (19.1cm)

1 **BASE INSIDE.** Use 6' (1.8m) of thread to work a strip of right-angle weave:

Unit 1 String 16A, leaving a 6" (15.2cm) tail. Tie a knot to form a circle and pass through the first 5A strung.

Unit 2 String 6A and pass through the 4A last exited and the first 5A just strung.

Unit 3 String 12A and pass through the 4A last exited and the first 8A just strung (FIGURE 1).

Repeat Units 2 and 3 until the strip is long enough to wrap the thickest part of your hand.

CONNECT Bring the ends of the strip together. String 1A and pass through the 4A at the beginning of the bracelet. String 1A and pass through the 4A at the end of the bracelet to complete the right-angle-weave unit (FIGURE 2).

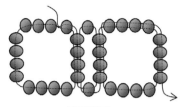

FIGURE 1

FIGURE 2

2 **BASE TOP AND BOTTOM.** Weave through beads to exit from 4A at the top of the strip. Work rounds of right-angle weave off the base inside to make 3 rows:

Unit 1 String 13A; pass through the 4A last exited and the first 4A just added (FIGURE 3).

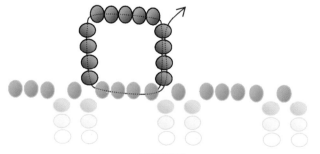

FIGURE 3

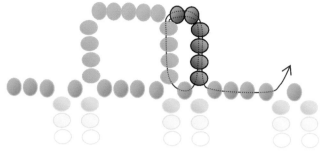

FIGURE 4

Unit 2 String 6A; pass through the top 1A of the next unit on the base inside, the side 4A of the previous unit in this round, the 6A just added, and the top 4A of the following unit on the base inside (FIGURE 4).

Unit 3 String 9A; pass through the side 4A of the previous unit and the top 4A last exited on the base inside. Pass through the first 4A just added (FIGURE 5).

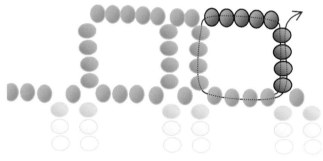

FIGURE 5

Repeat Units 2 and 3 around the base inside. Connect the round with 2A.

Weave through the beads to exit from 4A at the other edge of the base inside. Repeat this step to add another round of right-angle weave.

3 **BASE OUTSIDE.** Weave through beads to exit 5A at the base's edge. Bring the long edges of the base top and bottom together. Incorporate the edge beads to right-angle weave a fourth side.

Unit 1 String 5A; pass through the mirror 5A on the edge of the base top and pull tight. String 5A; pass through the 5A last exited on the base bottom, the first 5A added in this unit, and the top 5A on the base top. Pass through the second set of 5A added in this unit and the 2A at the top of the next unit on the edge of the base bottom.

Unit 2 String 5A; pass through the mirror 2A on the base top, the side 5A of the previous unit, the 2A first exited on the base bottom, the 5A just added, and the top 5A of the following base top unit (FIGURE 7).

FIGURE 7

Unit 3 String 5A; pass through the mirror 5A on the base bottom, the side 5A of the previous unit, the 5A first exited on the base top, the 5A just added, and the top 2A of the following base bottom unit. Repeat Units 2 and 3 to close the entire base into a four-sided tube. Connect the end units by weaving a right-angle thread path between the first 5A and last 5A added (FIGURE 8).

FIGURE 8

4 **BUMPS.** Work tubular even-count peyote-stitched "bumps" off the large base top and base bottom units:

Round 1 Weave through beads to exit between the fourth and fifth bead on a 5A side of a base top unit. String 1B and pass through the middle 2A of the next side in the unit; repeat to add a total of 4B. Step up for the next round by passing through the first 1B added in this round (FIGURE 9).

Round 2 String 2B and pass through the next 1B from Round 1; repeat to add a total of 8B. Step up through the first 2B added in this round (FIGURE 10).

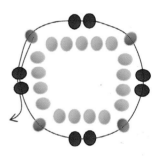

FIGURE 9   FIGURE 10

Round 3 String 1B and pass through the next 2B from Round 2; repeat to add a total of 4B. Step up through the first 1B added in this round (FIGURES 11 AND 12).

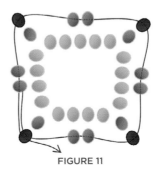

FIGURE 11   FIGURE 12

Round 4 String 1C and pass through the next 1B from Round 3; repeat around to add a total of 4C. Step up through the first 1C added in this round (FIGURE 13). Pass through the 4C two times to cinch the beads.

Repeat this step to embellish all of the large units along the base top and base bottom.

5 **RAYS.** Work rounds of tubular even-count peyote off the base outside.

Round 1 Weave through beads to exit between the fourth and fifth bead on a 5A side of a base outside unit. String 1A and pass through the second 1A of the next side in the unit (FIGURE 14); repeat around to add a total of 8A. Step up through the first bead added in this round (FIGURE 15).

Rounds 2–22 Work 21 rounds of tubular peyote stitch using 1 bead in each stitch. Step up for each round by passing through the first bead added in the round (FIGURE 16). Follow the color pattern below to blend from A to B to D. Work the beads listed for each round in random order to achieve a natural look:

Round 2 7A and 1B	**Round 18** 4B and 4D
Round 3 7A and 1B	**Round 19** 3B and 5D
Round 4 6A and 2B	**Round 20** 2B and 6D
Round 5 6A and 2B	**Round 21** 1B and 7D
Round 6 5A and 3B	**Round 22** 8D
Round 7 5A and 3B	**Round 23** String 1D and pass
Round 8 4A and 4B	through the next 2D from
Round 9 4A and 4B	the previous round to make a
Round 10 3A and 5B	decrease (FIGURE 17); repeat
Round 11 3A and 5B	to add a total of 4D. Step up
Round 12 2A and 6B	for the next round by passing
Round 13 1A and 7B	through the first decrease
Round 14 1A and 7B	beads, then through the
Round 15 7B and 1D	second bead added in this
Round 16 6B and 2D	round (FIGURE 18).
Round 17 5B and 3D	

FIGURE 13

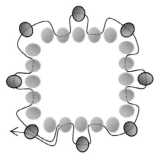

FIGURE 14

FIGURE 15

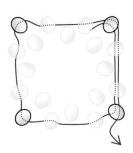

FIGURE 16

Round 24 String 1C and pass through the next D from the previous round; repeat to add a total of 4C. Step up through first bead added in this round. Pass through the next D from the previous round, then pass through the 4C of this round several times to cinch the beads together for a tidy finish (FIGURE 19).

Repeat this step to add a ray to each base outside unit.

FIGURE 17

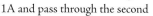

FIGURE 18

FIGURE 19

Short Variations

You can change the look of this bangle by shortening or lengthening the rays. This is the "Shortus" version to give you an idea of how it's done. For my variations, I used the following beads and adapted the instructions after Rays, Round 1.

SHORTUS
ADAPTED SEED BEAD AMOUNTS
16 g aqua size 11° seed beads (A)
7 g opaque white 11° seed beads (B)
6 g metallic bronze size 11° seed beads (D)

ADAPTED RAYS
Round 2 7A and 1D
Round 3 6A and 2D
Round 4 5A and 3D
Round 5 4A and 4D
Round 6 3A and 5D
Round 7 2A and 6D
Round 8 1A and 7D
Round 9 8D
Round 10 every other decrease with 4D
Round 11 4C

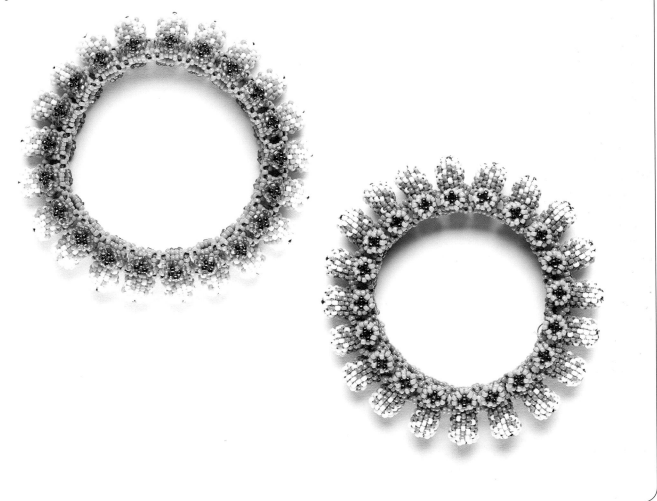

Long Variations

You can change the look of this bangle by shortening or lengthening the rays. This is the "Longus" version to give you an idea of how it's done. For my variations, I used the following beads and adapted the instructions after Rays, Round 1.

LONGUS
ADAPTED SEED BEAD AMOUNTS
34 g opaque orange size 11° seed beads (A)

26 g silver-lined peach size 11° seed beads (B)

4 g metallic silver size 11° seed beads (C)

13 g opaque white size 11° seed beads (D)

ADAPTED RAYS
Round 2 7A and 1B
Round 3 7A AND 1B
Round 4 7A AND 1B
Round 5 6A AND 2B
Round 6 6A AND 2B
Round 7 6A AND 2B
Round 8 5A AND 3B
Round 9 5A AND 3B
Round 10 5A AND 3B
Round 11 4A AND 4B
Round 12 4A AND 4B
Round 13 4A AND 4B
Round 14 3A AND 5B
Round 15 3A AND 5B
Round 16 3A AND 5B
Round 17 2A AND 6B
Round 18 2A AND 6B
Round 19 2A AND 6B
Round 20 1A AND 7B
Round 21 1A AND 7B

Round 22 1A AND 7B
Round 23 7B and 1D
Round 24 7B and 1D
Round 25 6B and 2D
Round 26 6B and 2D
Round 27 5B and 3D
Round 28 5B and 3D
Round 29 4B and 4D
Round 30 4B and 4D
Round 31 3B and 5D
Round 32 3B and 5D
Round 33 2B and 6D
Round 34 2B and 6D
Round 35 1B and 7D
Round 36 1B and 7D
Round 37 8D
Round 38 every other decrease with 4D
Round 39 4C

SEA STAR
at-a-glance

1 Base connection

2 Base top, Unit 1

3 Base top, Unit 2

4 Base top, Unit 3

5 Base top and bottom, finished

6 Base outside, Unit 1

7 Base outside, Unit 2

8 Base completed

9 Bumps, Round 1 step up

10 Bumps, Round 2 step up

11 Bumps, Round 3 step up

12 Bumps, Round 4 step up

⓭ Bumps completed

⓮ Rays, Round 1 step up

⓯ Rays, Round 2 step up

⓰ Rays, Round 23, first stitch

⓱ Rays, Round 24, cinching beads

This project is a good warm up to or cool down from making one of the other larger Ootheca-themed projects. This cheery bracelet design uses mainly size 8° seed beads so it works up quickly, and the shimmering bicone crystals add just enough sparkle to keep you entranced.

WHAT'S THE STORY?

At a weekend-long beadweaving retreat for new beaders near my home, we made swatches of many beadweaving stitches. After introducing right-angle weave, I continued stitching with the size 8° seed beads used for the demonstration and out came the base of this project. I thought, "here is this great base, so why not add some Ootheca bumps and a few crystals?" Before the end of the day, this quick bracelet had practically worked up on its own!

TECHNIQUES
Right-angle weave
Tubular peyote stitch
Attaching jump rings
See pages 122–140 for helpful technique information.

MATERIALS
12 g fuchsia size 8° seed beads (A)
3 g silver-lined ruby size 11° seed beads (B)
1 g chartreuse size 11° seed beads (C)
9 jet 2xAB 4mm crystal bicones
2 sterling silver 1x4mm tubes
6 sterling silver 5.5mm 20- or 18-gauge jump rings
1 sterling silver 7mm 20- or 18-gauge soldered jump ring
1 sterling silver 10x14mm lobster clasp
Gray or smoke beading thread

TOOLS
Size 12 beading needles
Thread snips or small scissors
2 pairs of chain-nose pliers

FINISHED SIZE
7½" (19.1cm)

RACHEL'S TIP

→ A great source for sterling silver 1x4mm tubes is "liquid silver"—the beads traditionally used for strung multistrand Native American necklaces.

1 BASE. Use single thread and A to right-angle weave a bracelet base:

Unit 1 String 16A; tie a square knot to form a tight circle and pass through the first 4A to clear the knot.

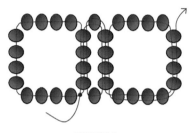

FIGURE 1

Unit 2 String 6A; pass through the 4A last exited and the first 5A just added.

Unit 3 String 12A; pass through the 4A last exited and the first 8A just added (FIGURE 1).

Units 4–18 Repeats Units 2 and 3 for a total of 18 units or to your desired length (FIGURE 2).

FIGURE 2

2 BUMPS. Weave through beads to exit between the third and fourth A on one side of the final base unit. Work tubular peyote-stitched "bumps" off the large base units:

Round 1 String 1A and pass through middle 2A of the next side in the same unit; repeat to add a total of 4A. Step up through the first 1A added in this round (FIGURE 3).

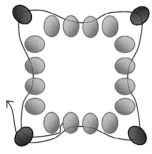

FIGURE 3

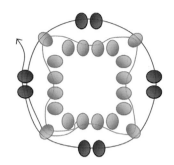

FIGURE 4

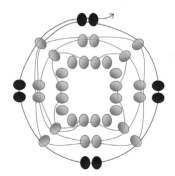

FIGURE 5

Round 2 String 2A and pass through the next 1A from Round 1; repeat to add a total of 8A. Step up through the first 2A added in this round (FIGURES 4 AND 5).

Round 3 String 1A and pass through the next set of 2A from Round 2; repeat to add a total of 4A. Step up through the first 1A added in this round (FIGURES 6 AND 7).

Round 4 String 2B and pass through the next 1A from Round 3; repeat to add a total of 8B. Step up through the first 2B added in this round (FIGURE 8).

Round 5 String 1B and pass through the next set of 2B from Round 4; repeat to add a total of 4B. Step up through the first 1B added in this round (FIGURE 9).

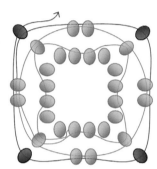

FIGURE 6

FIGURE 7

FIGURE 8

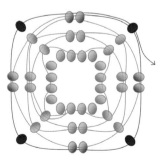

FIGURE 9

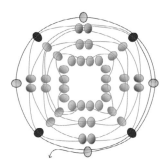

FIGURE 10

FIGURE 11

Round 6 String 1C and pass through the next 1B from Row 5; repeat to add a total of 4C. Step up through the first 1C added in this round. Pass through the next 1B from Round 5 and the next 1C (FIGURE 10). Pass through all 4C several times to close the top of the tube (FIGURE 11).

3 CRYSTALS. Weave through beads to exit the bottom 1A of the next base unit. String 1B, 1 bicone, and 1B; pass through the top 1A of the base unit. String 1B and pass back through the crystal. String 1B and pass through the bottom 1A of the base unit. Repeat the thread path 1 or 2 more times to secure (FIGURE 12).

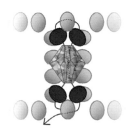

FIGURE 12

Repeat Steps 2 and 3 down the length of the bracelet.

4 ENDS. Weave through beads to exit from 1A (an "up bead") at the bracelet's end. String 1B, 1 sterling silver tube, and 1B and pass into the opposing 1A up bead. Weave through these beads several times to reinforce. Repeat at other end of bracelet.

Use two 5.5mm jump rings to attach the lobster clasp to the silver tube at the one end of the bracelet.

Attach two 5.5mm jump rings to the silver tube at the other end of the bracelet. Use two 5.5mm jump rings to attach the jump rings just placed to the 7mm jump ring (FIGURE 13).

FIGURE 13

Mini O. Bracelet—
"Brown" variation

MINI O.
at-a-glance

1 Unit 1

2 Unit 2

3 Unit 3

4 Base

5 Bumps, Round 1, first stitch

6 Bumps, Round 1 step up

7 Bumps, Round 2, first stitch

8 Bumps, Round 2 step up

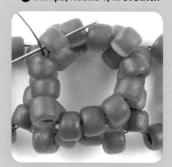

9 Bumps, Round 3 step up

10 Bumps, Round 4 step up

11 Bumps, Round 5 step up

12 Bumps, Round 6 step up for closing tube

13 Bumps, closed top

14 Crystal start point

15 Crystal attachment point

16 Crystal reentry

17 Crystal completed

18 End attachment point

19 End completed

20 Clasp

21 Rings

A simple façade belies a right-angle-weave pattern worthy of your concerted attention. Each component is made separately, then strung together on elastic to form a comfortable and stunning bracelet.

WHAT'S THE STORY?

When I'm at a loss for a design's title or can't decide on one, I'll sometimes ask other beaders, family, or friends what the piece reminds them of. When this question was posed to my husband regarding this piece, he said without hesitation that each component looked like a crown, which hadn't occurred to me! Add an "O" for *Ootheca* and the title was complete.

TECHNIQUES
Right-angle weave
Tubular peyote stitch
Ending and starting thread
See pages 122–140 for helpful technique information.

MATERIALS
30 g opaque lavender size 11° seed beads (A)
25 g matte root beer AB size 11° seed beads (B)
5 g white opal size 11° seed beads (C)
5 g sapphire luster size 11° seed beads (D)
100 vitrial 3mm crystal bicones
50 mottled light brown 6x4mm faceted pressed-glass rondelles
Gray or smoke beading thread
4' (1.2m) of clear elastic floss
Clear jeweler's cement

TOOLS
Thread snips or small scissors
Size 12 English beading needles
Wide-eye needle

FINISHED SIZE
6¼" (15.9cm)

RACHEL'S TIP

→ It's a good idea to weave through the right-angle-weave base one more time for extra strength, as long as the bead holes are large enough.

1 BASE. Use single thread, A and B, and right-angle weave to create a right-angle-weave base as shown in **FIGURE 1A**.

Row 1 String 11A and tie a square knot to form a tight circle, leaving a 6" (15.2cm) tail. Pass through the first 3A to clear the knot. String 5A; pass through the 3A last exited and the first 4A just added. String 8A; pass through the 3A last exited and the first 5A just added. String 5A; pass through the 3A last exited and the first 4A just added. String 8A; pass through the 3A last exited and the first 2A just added.

Row 2 String 2A, 1B, and 2A; pass through the 2A last exited, the 5 beads just added, and the adjacent bottom bead of the next Row 1 unit. String 2A and 1B; pass through the side 2A of the previous unit, the bottom bead of the adjacent Row 1 unit, and the 2A just added. String 1B and 2A; pass through the 2A at the bottom of the next Row 1 unit, the 2A last exited, the 3 beads just added, and the adjacent bottom bead of the next Row 1 unit. String 2A and 1B; pass through the side of 2A of the previous unit, the bottom bead of the adjacent Row 1 unit, and the 2A just added. String 1B and 2A; pass through the 2A at the bottom of the final Row 1 unit, the 2A last exited, and the 1B just added.

Row 3 Use 1B on each side as you work 5 units of right-angle weave off the B added in Row 2. Exit from the bottom 1B of the last unit added in this row.

Row 4 String 6A; pass through the 1B last exited, the 6A just added,

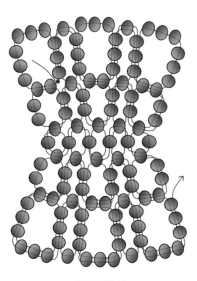

FIGURE 1A

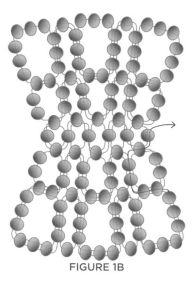

FIGURE 1B

and the 1B at the bottom of the next Row 3 unit. String 3A; pass through the 2A last exited, the 1B at the bottom of the adjacent Row 3 unit, and the first 2A just added. String 4A; pass through the 1B at the bottom of the next Row 3 unit, the 2A last exited, the 4A just added, and the 1B at the bottom of the following Row 3 unit. String 3A; pass through the 2A last exited, the 1B at the bottom of the adjacent Row 3 unit, and the first 2A just added. String 4A; pass through the 1B at the bottom of the next Row 3 unit, the 2A last exited, and the first 2A just added.

Row 5 String 9A; pass through the 2A last exited, the 9A just added, and the 1A at the bottom of the next Row 4 unit. String 4A; pass through the side 3A of the previous unit, the 1A at the bottom of the adjacent Row 4 unit, and the first 3A just added. String 6A; pass through the 2A at the bottom of the next Row 4 unit, the side 3A of the previous unit, the 6A just added, and the 1A at the bottom of the following Row 4 unit. String 4A; pass through the side 3A of the previous unit, the 1A at the bottom of the adjacent Row 4 unit, and the first 3A just added. String 6A; pass through the 2A at the bottom of the next Row 4 unit and weave through beads to exit 1B at the edge of Row 3 (**FIGURE 1B**).

2 SIDES. Fold the base in half so Rows 1 and 5 touch. Use B to right-angle weave the units together:

Right Pass up through 2A at the edge of Row 2. String 1B; pass down through the edge 2A of Row 4, the edge 1B of Row 3,

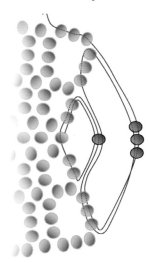

FIGURE 2

FIGURE 3

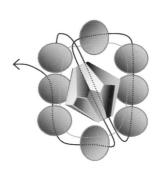

FIGURE 6

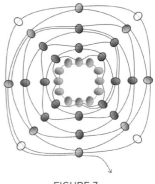

FIGURE 7

up through the edge 2A of Row 2, the 1B just added, and up through the edge 3A of Row 5. String 3B; pass down through the edge 3A of Row 1, the first 1B added in this step, up through the edge 3A of Row 5, the 3A just added, and through the 3A at the top of the first Row 5 unit (FIGURE 2).

Top In the same manner, connect the top of the Row 1 units to the bottom of the Row 5 units using 3B in each stitch (FIGURE 3).

Left Repeat the right side in reverse.

3 CRYSTALS AND BUMPS. Embellish the base with alternating crystal and tubular peyote- stitched "bumps":

Side crystal Exiting the last 1B added, string 1 bicone. Pass through the unit's 3B, adjacent 3A, the crystal, and 2B (FIGURE 4).

Short bump String 1B and pass through the middle bead of the next side in the unit; repeat 3 more times for a total of 4B. Step up through the first 1B added. Repeat to stitch 3 more rounds using B and 1 round using C (FIGURE 5). Pass through the adjacent 1B of the previous round and the next 1C. Pass through the 4C two times to close the top of the bump. Weave through beads to exit 3B of the next top unit on the base.

Top crystal String 1 bicone. Pass through the unit's opposite side 3B and top 1B, back through the crystal, and through the bottom 1B. Weave through adjacent 2B (FIGURE 6).

Tall bump Work as you did the short bump, this time with 4 rounds of B, 2 rounds of D, and 1 round of C (FIGURE 7).

Finish the component by adding 1 more top crystal, 1 more short bump, and 1 more side crystal. Secure the thread and trim; set aside. Repeat this step for a total of 25 components.

4 ASSEMBLY. Thread the wide-eye needle with doubled stretch cord. Pass through the center of the right-angle-weave units under the right bump of 1 component; string 1 rondelle. Repeat the stringing sequence to connect all the components' right sides. Snug the beads and components, tie several square knots to secure the cord, and trim. Place a small amount of glue on the knot. Repeat to string the left side of the components.

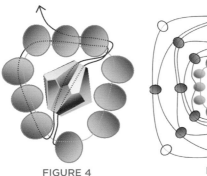

FIGURE 4   **FIGURE 5**

O. Crown Cuff—
"Katherine" variation

O. CROWN
at-a-glance

❶ Base, Row 1, first unit

❷ Base, Row 1, second unit

❸ Base, Row 1 complete

❹ Base, Row 2, beginning first unit

❺ Base, Row 2, completing first unit

❻ Base, Row 2, beginning second unit

❼ Base, Row 2, completing second unit

❽ Base, Row 2, third unit

❾ Base, Row 2, fourth unit

❿ Base, Row 2, fifth unit

⓫ Base, Row 3

⓬ Base, Row 4

⓭ Base completed

⑭ Side, first unit on right

⑮ Side, second unit on right

⑯ Side, first unit on top

⑰ Side, second unit on top

⑱ Side, first unit on left

⑲ Crystal

⑳ Short bump, first stitch

㉑ Short bump, first round step up

㉒ Short bump, closed top

㉓ Top crystal

㉔ Tall bump

BASICS

In this chapter, I'll share information on the specific materials, tools, and techniques that are brought together to form each of these 18 unique projects. You'll find that the materials descriptions include some of my own preferences. And while many of the steps for each project are contained within each set of project directions, I've also included basic information on bead stitches, wireworking, and general jewelry making, so you can check back here with any questions.

Gathering Your Materials and Tools

If you're new to beading or wirework, gathering the materials and tools for the projects in *Seed Bead Fusion* will be a new shopping adventure! There are lots of books on jewelry making out there, so please consider this book a successor to earlier books that list more comprehensive information about beads and other jewelers' materials. Rather than re-hash information already printed ad infinitum, I've just included a brief description of each bead and material used here. If you're interested in learning more, you can find a wealth of information by joining a bead group, searching online, or visiting your local library.

BEADS

A bead is anything one might put a needle or wire into and out of, though our determination of "bead" is applied more specifically for our purposes here. While they come in an infinite spectrum by the first definition, for ease of duplicating what is seen in these pages, a narrowed definition is applied. Since you've made it this far into the pages of information and photos, there is at least a small something which draws you to these small beautiful things.

SEED BEADS are small glass beads available in a dizzying array of colors, shapes, and sizes. I mostly use Japanese seed beads because they have large holes for many passes, their colors are consistent from lot to lot, and their color choice far exceeds seed beads manufactured in other countries. I mainly use size 11° round seed beads, with a few of the smaller size 15° round seed beads and larger size 8° round seed beads sprinkled in. I also like to use 3.4mm Japanese drop beads.

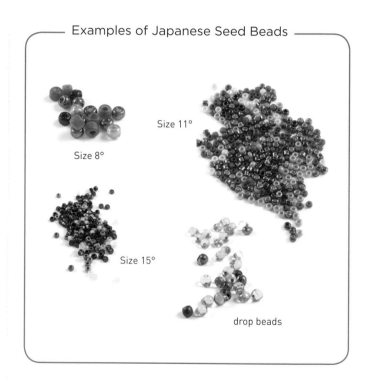

Examples of Japanese Seed Beads

Size 8°

Size 11°

Size 15°

drop beads

CRYSTAL BEADS, made with lead crystal, are renowned for their incredible sparkle, and personally, I can't get enough. You'll find crystal beads, crystal pearls, and rivolis in this book.

CZECH GLASS BEADS are readily available in a wide variety of fire-polished and pressed types and offer a little sparkle and a nice price.

FRESHWATER PEARLS are naturally made beads that offer economic luxury.

LIQUID SILVER BEADS are tiny tubes of sterling silver. They are traditionally strung into the many-strand necklaces you sometimes see in Native American jewelry. In this book, I've used them as findings.

MATERIALS FOR YOUR WORKTABLE

Because beads do not assemble on their own, you'll also need a few materials to give your pieces shape and strength.

THREAD is a personal choice for off-loom work, but I recommend using Silamide A or FireLine 6- and 8-pound test for the projects in *Seed Bead Fusion*. I prefer gray to other colors in most cases because it hides in the shadows nicely.

THREAD TREATMENT is applied to your thread to help heighten tension or lubrication within your beadwork. I prefer to use natural beeswax on my projects, if any treatment at all.

FLEXIBLE BEADING WIRE is comprised of multiple strands of stainless steel encased in nylon. You connect this type of wire to a finding by stringing on and clamping down a crimp bead at each end of the piece (see *Crimping*, page 126).

WIRE is defined by type of material (copper, sterling silver, gold, base metal), gauge (the higher the gauge number, the thinner the wire), and hardness (dead-soft, half-hard, and hard). I use dead-soft wire in almost all of the projects except ear wires, which call for half-hard wire. I mainly use 26- through 18-gauge wire.

STRETCH CORD is an elastic stringing material. I prefer the fibrous Gossamer Floss stitched with a Big Eye needle.

FINDINGS are the small parts, usually metal, that hold jewelry together. *Jump rings* and *split rings* are used to link findings and can be purchased or handmade (see *Jump Rings*, page 132). *Clasps* are added to the ends of a piece of jewelry as a closure. I use lobster, toggle, and S-clasps but am also quite fond of using magnetic clasps and buttons. Another type of finding to add to your selection is *ear wires*—simple wire hooks that attach to pierced ears (see *Ear Wires*, page 132).

Size 12 beading needles

NEEDLES are used to pass thread through bead holes. It's important to use fine needles or those intended for beadwork. Size 12 beading needles come with the ability to pass through bead holes several times. While "sharps" may also be used, they are thicker and minimize the number of thread passes. Use a Big Eye needle for stringing beads onto thicker thread such as gossamer floss or when beadweaving with large-holed beads.

LIGHTING helps to differentiate between subtly similar colors and makes bead holes more apparent. I have a folding lamp with a full-spectrum bulb at each of my three different beading locations. While incandescent bulbs might be illuminating, they cast a yellow hue, resulting in untrue color.

MAGNIFICATION is there for us when our eyes falter. If we want to keep beading, we must magnify! Or, as my optometrist recommends, make a visit to your eye doctor if the bead holes are eluding you.

BEADING MATS serve as your beading surface, keeping your beads and other items at rest until they're ready to be incorporated into the beadwork. I prefer to use a large gray or black velvet board in the studio and a foldable square of Vellux fabric when traveling.

Chain-nose pliers

Flat-nose pliers

Wireworking Tools

Learning as much as you can about wireworking tools will help you become an excellent jewelry maker. If you're just starting out, you'll find the choices are vast as far as type and quality. It'll be tempting at first to purchase economy tools, but I recommend beginning with mid-market German-made tools and then working your way up a little at a time. I often work with a mix of tool qualities to suit the task at hand. For example, if my project requires larger wire, I reach for my German-made or Swanstrom tools. For projects that include detailed wirework, I grab my high-quality Lindstrom and Tronex tools.

A secondary concern regarding jewelry-making tools is whether or not there is an internal spring to repel the two parts of the tool. This ergonomic consideration is very important to minimize the physical demand on your hand, reducing the chance of injury in the long run. While spring-free tools allow greater control because your hand does both the opening and closing rather than a spring, I use spring tools, as the risks outweigh the benefits. Whether your pliers have springs or not, take care to work in 30-minute to 1-hour increments and take time in between to vary your tasks or stretch your arms, wrists, neck, and shoulders.

Round-nose pliers

Flat round-nose pliers

Flush cutters

Super flush cutters

CHAIN-NOSE PLIERS have smooth jaws with small angular tips. They are used to manipulate wire and other jewelry-making items such as jump rings and sometimes crimp beads and are also helpful for pulling a beading needle through a tight spot. They are often mistakenly called "needle-nose pliers," which is a completely different tool with extra-long jaws.

FLAT-NOSE PLIERS are smooth-jawed with wide bill-like tips. They provide an excellent grip on wire and are particularly useful when creating spirals. You can also use them as a partner to chain-nose pliers to open and close jump rings without leaving a mark on the jump rings.

ROUND-NOSE PLIERS have two equally round tapered tips and are used for making round wire loops. Be careful when using these for any other task, as they leave marks in the metal at each gripping point.

FLAT ROUND-NOSE PLIERS have one flat bill-like jaw, like a flat-nose pliers, and one round jaw, like a round-nose pliers. This type of pliers is used for making curves and jump rings. They can almost always replace the duties of round-nose pliers, with the added benefit of leaving a minimized dent in the wire. They are particularly useful for coiling up a small batch of jump rings.

FLUSH CUTTERS AND SUPER FLUSH CUTTERS are used for cutting wire. When you cut with this type of tool, one wire end is flat, or flush, and the other end is pointed (see *Flush Cutting*, page 127). Wirework with flush-cut ends is tidier and has an overall appeal. The good news is that flush cutters aren't necessarily more expensive. The difference between the two type of tools has to do with the quality of the cut. While either tool cuts what appears to be flush from an arm's length, they differ when viewed closely. The flush-wire-end cut with flush cutters retains a small bur of wire down the middle. The flush-wire-end cut with super flush or razor flush cutters comes much closer to truly being flush.

WIRE STRAIGHTENERS, also known as *nylon-jaw flat-nose pliers* or *nylon-jaw pliers*, have wide nylon jaws. They are used for taking the kinks out of bent wire. Just use the pliers to pinch and pull the wire straight and you're one step closer to more finished-looking work (see *Straightening Wire*, page 127). If you're into German or higher quality tools, rest easy, this economic tool is built to last.

Wire straighteners

Jewelry-making Basics

I've used several basic jewelry-making methods to finish the projects in *Seed Bead Fusion*. Each technique is super simple and yet essential.

CRIMPING

This method for bead stringing is by far the easiest, strongest, and most widely used technique by people making jewelry as a hobby, as well as those designing jewelry for a living.

1 Cut a piece of flexible beading wire the length of finished piece, plus 4" (10.2cm).

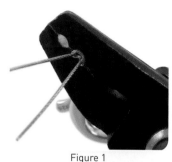

2 String one 2×2mm crimp bead and one half of a clasp. Pass back through the crimp bead, leaving a 1" (2.5cm) tail. Tighten the loop so it is snug but can move freely along the clasp loop.

3 Position the crimping pliers so the smooth divot of the back notch is on the bottom. Grasp the crimp bead in the pliers' back notch. Firmly squeeze the crimp bead so it forms a U shape (FIGURE 1).

Figure 1

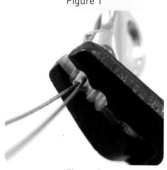

Figure 2

4 Hold the crimp bead in the front notch (FIGURE 2) and squeeze the bead, collapsing it into a tube.

5 String beads onto the wire. Repeat Steps 2–4 to finish the other end of the strand. Tuck any excess wire into the nearest bead holes.

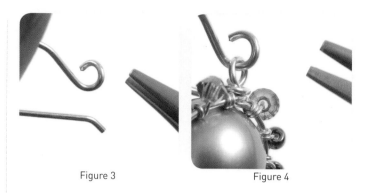

Figure 3   Figure 4

ATTACHING EAR WIRES

To make an earring, add an ear wire to a dangle using chain-nose pliers.

1 With the chain-nose pliers in your dominant hand, grasp the ear-wire loop and press it forward (FIGURE 3).

2 String 1 earring dangle and use the tips of chain-nose pliers to close the loop in the opposite way you opened it (FIGURE 4).

Figure 5   Figure 6

ATTACHING JUMP RINGS

Join components together with jump rings using two chain-nose pliers. For extra strength, use two jump rings or one thicker-gauge jump ring.

1 Use the tip of chain-nose pliers to hold half of the jump ring with the ring's opening on top (FIGURE 5).

2 Open the jump ring by grasping the other side of the ring with a second pair of chain-nose pliers and pressing forward (FIGURE 6).

3 Attach your component to the open jump ring and use the second pair of chain-nose pliers to close the ring in the opposite way you opened it.

Wireworking Basics

If you're already working with wire, great! If not, you're in for a treat because I've got news for you—working with wire is actually easy once you're armed with a few tips and a little practice with the right tools and materials. Follow along as I show you how to do the basic wireworking techniques used in the projects in this book.

USING FLAT ROUND-NOSE PLIERS

I've used standard beads, tools, and materials in this book, but one exception is the use of round-nose pliers throughout, when sometimes flat round-nose pliers would yield superior results. Please see *Flat Round-nose Pliers*, page 125, to learn when it's the best time to use this type of tool.

Figure 10

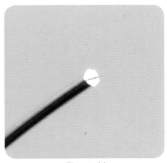

Figure 11

Figure 7

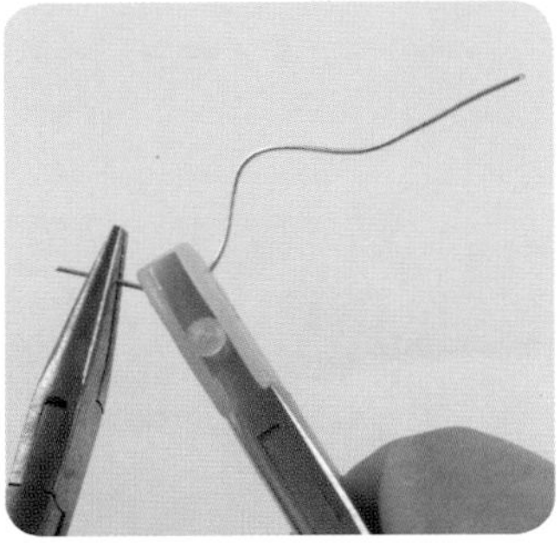

Figure 8

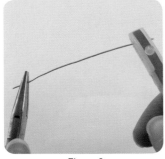

Figure 9

STRAIGHTENING WIRE

Ever think that if wirework were just a little easier, you might get more into it? Upon witnessing a demonstration of wire-straightening pliers, I've seen strict beadweavers set straight!

1 Use your nondominant hand to grasp one end of the bent wire with chain-nose pliers (FIGURE 7).

2 Use your dominant hand to grasp the wire with wire straighteners near the chain-nose pliers (FIGURE 8).

3 Clamp down with the wire straighteners and pull to the end of the wire. Repeat as needed to get a shiny, straight piece of wire (FIGURE 9).

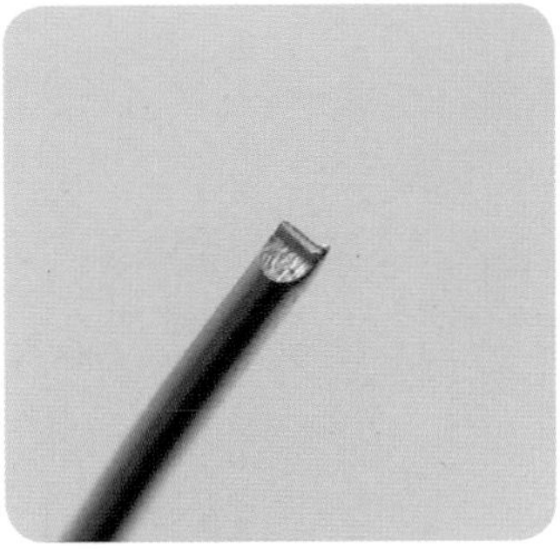

Figure 12

FLUSH CUTTING

Performing a flat, or *flush*, cut at the end of heavy-gauge wire cleans up the look of a piece in a small and important way. While not required, it gives the piece a professional finish. A *flush cutter* or *super flush cutter* is required to perform a flush cut (see *Flush cutters*, page 125).

1 Position the flush cutter to cut off only about 1mm of pointed wire with the flat side of the cutter pointing toward the side of the wire you'll be keeping (FIGURE 10).

2 The wire on the flat side of the cutters will become flat (FIGURE 11).

3 The wire on the divot side of the cutter will be pointed (FIGURE 12).

BASIC LOOP

This technique creates an open loop that's appropriate for thicker wires such as 20- and 18-gauge.

1 With the wire (or the work) in your nondominant hand and round-nose pliers in your dominant hand, hold the very tip of the flush-cut wire (see *Flush Cutting*, above) with the point of the round-nose pliers. You can position your grasp anywhere along the jaws to get a variety of loop sizes. Grip the wire as you coil the end away from yourself one quarter turn (FIGURE 13).

Figure 13

Figure 14

Figure 15

Figure 16

2 Open the pliers' jaws while leaving one of the jaws inside the bend. Rotate the outside jaw of the pliers back toward you and grip the wire once again (FIGURE 14).

3 Coil the wire one quarter turn away from you until the wire end reaches the main wire (FIGURE 15).

4 To make a double basic loop or coil end, continue tightly wrapping the wire until there are 2 complete revolutions (FIGURE 16).

CONSISTENT LOOPS

Consider using a permanent marker to draw a perpendicular line on the jaws of your round-nose pliers at the point at which you turn your first loop. When you make subsequent loops you can make them at this mark so all your loops will be the same width.

WRAPPED LOOP

Employ wrapped loops for extra security—these babies are not opening up! The projects in this book mostly employ 22-gauge wire loops, but they may also be made with larger gauges for extra security or smaller gauges for small bead holes.

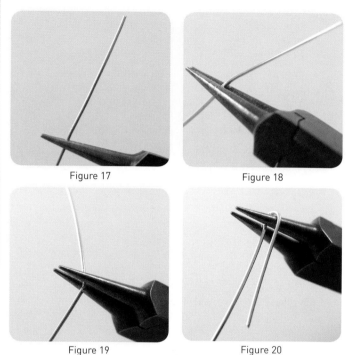

Figure 17

Figure 18

Figure 19

Figure 20

1 Grasp the wire with the tip of round-nose pliers, 1" (2.5cm) from the end (FIGURE 17).

2 Use your fingers to press the 1" (2.5cm) of wire over the top of one of the pliers' jaws to make a 45° bend (FIGURE 18).

3 Adjust the pliers to hold just above the new bend at the appropriate loop size on the pliers' jaws (FIGURE 19).

4 Use your fingers to bend the 1" (2.5cm) wire up, around, and down the side of the pliers' top jaw (FIGURE 20).

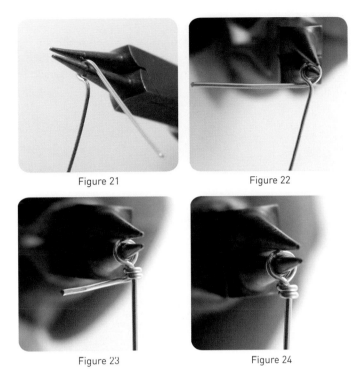

Figure 21

Figure 22

Figure 23

Figure 24

5 Adjust the pliers so the bottom jaw is in the loop (FIGURE 21).

6 With the pliers still in the loop, use your fingers to swing the 1" (2.5cm) wire under and toward you to cross the main wire at 90° (FIGURE 22).

7 Use your fingers or chain-nose pliers to wrap the 1" (2.5cm) wire tightly around the main wire 2 times, beginning close to the loop (FIGURE 23).

8 Flush cut the tail wire close to the wrap (see *Flush Cutting*, page 127) (FIGURE 24).

WRAPPED-BEAD LINK OR DANGLE

This technique is used to secure a bead that's been strung on a head pin, eye pin, or wire that's been finished with another loop.

1 Use the tip of round-nose pliers to grasp the wire at the top of the bead. Use your fingers of the other hand to push the wire away from you over the pliers' jaw to make a 45° bend (FIGURE 25).

2 Adjust the position of the round-nose pliers so they hold the wire slightly above the 45° bend at the appropriate loop size on the pliers' jaws (FIGURE 26).

3 Use your fingers to bend the working wire up, around, and down the side of the pliers' top jaw (FIGURE 27).

4 Adjust the pliers so the bottom jaw is in the loop (FIGURE 28).

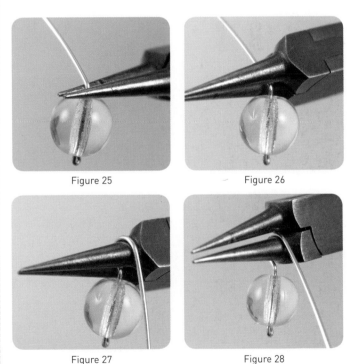

Figure 25

Figure 26

Figure 27

Figure 28

Figure 29

Figure 30

Figure 33

Figure 34

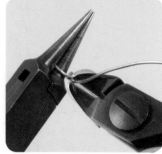

Figure 31

Figure 32

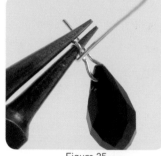

Figure 35

Figure 36

5 Use your fingers to swing the wire up to a 90° angle (FIGURE 29).

6 Use your fingers or chain-nose pliers to wrap the wire around itself under the loop (FIGURE 30).

7 Flush cut the tail wire close to the wrap (see *Flush Cutting*, page 127) (FIGURE 31).

8 Tuck in any remaining wire with the tip of chain-nose pliers (FIGURE 32).

Figure 37

BRIOLETTE WRAP

This loop-making method is used to create dangles with horizontally drilled beads like teardrop-shaped briolettes. Use thin wires such as 26- to 22-gauge.

1 Cut 3" (7.6cm) of wire. String the briolette so 1" (2.5cm) of wire extends from one side of the bead. Bring both wire ends up along the top of the bead so they become parallel. Give each wire a slight bend just above the briolette so they are as close together as possible (FIGURE 33).

2 Grasp the long wire end where the 2 wires meet. Use round-nose pliers to form a loop with the long wire end (FIGURE 34).

3 Adjust the pliers so the bottom jaw is in the loop. Wrap the long wire end around the short wire end with 2 tight coils (FIGURES 35 AND 36).

4 Bend the short wire 90° and flush cut the wire ends close to the wrap (see *Flush Cutting*, page 127) (FIGURE 37).

BEADED BRIOLETTE WRAP

This technique is the same as above but with an additional bead. Again, use 26- to 22-gauge wire for this method.

1 Cut 3" (7.6cm) of wire. String the briolette so 1" (2.5cm) of wire extends from one side of the bead. Bend the long side of the wire so it sticks straight up from the top of the bead. Bend the short wire so it crosses the long wire just above the briolette (FIGURE 38).

2 Wrap the short wire around the long wire with 2 tight coils. Flush cut the tail wire close to the coils (see *Flush Cutting*, page 127) (FIGURE 39).

3 String a bead on the long wire (FIGURE 40).

4 Form a wrapped loop to secure the bead (see *Wrapped Loop*, page 128) (FIGURE 41).

HEAD PINS

Head pins are used for holding beads on wire. This version is good for a variety of uses, and you'll find them in several projects in *Seed Bead Fusion*. It's a good technique to know because making your own head pins can be considerably less expensive than buying them commercially.

1 Flush cut the wire end (see *Flush Cutting*, page 127). Use the tip of chain-nose pliers to hold the tip of your wire end. Curl the wire away from you 180° degrees. The newly bent wire should run parallel to the original wire (FIGURE 42).

2 Use the wider part of chain-nose pliers to grasp the hook-shaped wire between the jaws (FIGURE 43).

3 Gently squeeze the pliers so the bent and main wires touch (FIGURE 44).

Figure 38

Figure 39

Figure 42

Figure 40

Figure 41

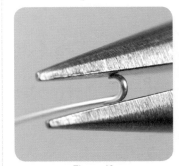
Figure 43

Figure 44

Figure 45

Figure 46

Figure 47

Figure 48

JUMP RINGS

This small finding is made up of a circle of wire with an opening and is used for connecting findings and loops to each other. Jump rings can be purchased premade, or you can make your own to custom fit. This is a good project to use flat round-nose pliers in place of round-nose pliers to minimize dents in the wire.

1 Create a coil (see *Coil End* [*Basic Loop*, Step 4], page 127) that's wrapped once more than the number of jump rings desired (FIGURE 45).

2 With the flat part of the flush cutter facing most of the coil and the divot side poised near the very end of the coil, snip off a small length of wire to give the coil's end a flush cut (FIGURE 46).

3 Flip the cutters in your hand so that the flat side is facing toward you. Align the cutters' tip as close as you can with the first cut and cut the next coil (FIGURE 47).

4 Once the ring is removed, the end of the coil will again be pointed. To continue creating jump rings, repeat from Step 2 (FIGURE 48).

Figure 49

Figure 50

Figure 51

Figure 52

EAR WIRES

Make these basic ear wires using 20- or 19-gauge round half-hard wire.

1 Flush cut 2" (5.1cm) of wire (see *Flush Cutting*, page 127) and form a basic loop (see *Basic Loop*, page 127). Place the loop against the body of a ballpoint pen, under the cap (FIGURE 49).

2 While pressing the pen cap's tab down, shape the wire around the pen body until it hits the loop (FIGURE 50).

3 Flush cut the wire below the point that's aligned with the bottom of the loop (FIGURE 51).

4 Use chain-nose pliers to bend the wire end for a finished look (FIGURE 52).

5 If needed, use a metal file or emery board to remove any burrs at the wire end (FIGURE 53).

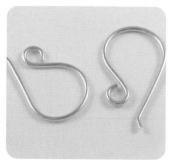

Figure 53

COILED S-CLASP

There's something special about making a handmade piece of jewelry from beginning to end, including the findings. Make this piece and forgo a commercial clasp.

1 Cut a 2' (61cm) piece of straightened 22-gauge wire (see *Straightening Wire*, page 127). Cross it over the top of 4" (10.2cm) of 18-gauge wire, 1" (2.5cm) from the wire end. Tightly wrap the 22-gauge wire around the 18-gauge a few times (FIGURE 54).

2 Continue wrapping the 22-gauge wire to form a 1" (2.5cm) coil. As the coil grows, slide it down the 18-gauge wire to the left. Use the wire straighteners if needed—it will help keep your coils tidy. Do all the coiling near the end of the 18-gauge wire. You'll have the most control over the coiling this way (FIGURE 55).

3 String 1 round 8mm bead onto the 18-gauge wire and slide it to the coil. Wrap the 22-gauge wire around the bead on its other side to keep it in place (FIGURE 56).

4 Continue wrapping the 22-gauge wire to form another 1" (2.5cm) coil (FIGURE 57).

Figure 58

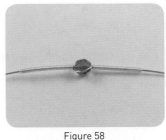

Figure 59

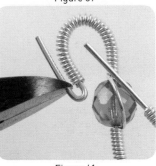

Figure 60

Figure 61

Figure 62

Figure 63

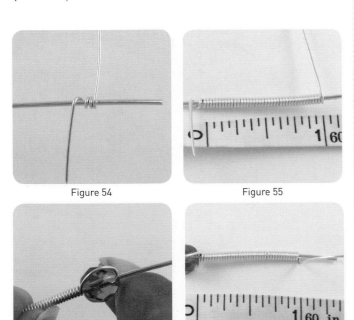

Figure 54

Figure 55

Figure 56

Figure 57

5 Flush cut the 22-gauge wire near the coil (see *Flush Cutting*, page 127) (FIGURE 58).

6 Use your fingers and pliers to individually bend the ends into an S shape (FIGURE 59).

7 Use the tip of chain-nose pliers to bend the 18-gauge wire 180° so the wire is parallel to itself, forming a hook shape (FIGURE 60).

8 Flush cut the 18-gauge wire so it's aligned with the coil end (FIGURE 61).

9 Use chain-nose pliers to squeeze the hook closed, ensuring that the clasp won't snag hair, skin, or clothing (FIGURE 62).

10 Repeat Steps 8 and 9 on the other end of the 18-gauge wire. Add large-sized 18-gauge jump rings to each side of the clasp (see *Jump Rings*, page 132) (FIGURE 63).

Off-loom Basics

At the heart of two-thirds of the projects in this book is a variety of beadweaving stitches. Each set of directions provides photos, illustrations, and text specific to the project. Refer to this section for a refresher on basics for each of the techniques.

STOP BEAD

Use a stop bead to keep beads from falling off the end of the thread when you first begin.

1 Prepare the working thread.

2 String 1 size 11° bead in a color not included in your project and let it slide to the end of the thread.

3 Tie an overhand knot around the bead and leave a 6" (15.2cm) tail to be worked into the beadwork later.

4 Once a portion of the beading is completed or if the working thread is getting too short to work with, remove the stop bead and work the thread into the beadwork.

HOW MUCH THREAD

The amount of thread you use for a project is a personal preference, but I like to use about 6' (1.8m) for general beadweaving. This is long enough so that I don't have to keep starting new thread but short enough so that the extra length doesn't get in my way or become tangled.

FLAT EVEN-COUNT PEYOTE STITCH

Flat peyote stitch is the most straight-forward variation of peyote stitch, a great technique for depicting graphed scenes or providing a flat surface for embellishment. This particular technique isn't included in the projects presented here, but it's worth mentioning to help you better understand some of the peyote-stitch variations used.

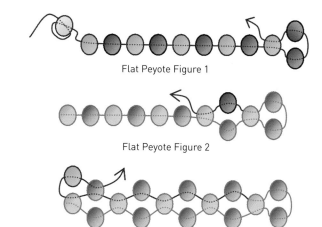

Flat Peyote Figure 1

Flat Peyote Figure 2

Flat Peyote Figure 3

1 Attach a stop bead (see *Stop Bead*, above left) to the end of 6' (1.8m) of thread and string an even number of beads. This strand makes up the first 2 rows.

2 String 1 bead and pass back through the second-to-last bead strung in the previous Step 1 (FLAT PEYOTE FIGURE 1).

3 String 1 bead, skip 1 bead, and pass through the next bead from previous row; repeat to the end of the row (FLAT PEYOTE FIGURE 2).

4 Step up to the next row by stringing 1 bead and passing back through the last bead added in the previous row (FLAT PEYOTE FIGURE 3). String 1 bead and pass through the following bead from previous row; repeat to the end of the row.

5 Repeat Steps 3 and 4 to the desired length.

ENDING AND STARTING THREAD IN PEYOTE STITCH

You may run out of thread while working peyote stitch. Read on to learn how to end a working thread and start a new one.

END THE THREAD (red line) by adding the final bead (shown in pink) and weaving diagonally through the existing beadwork for several rows. Stitch through 2 beads in a circle at least twice, weave diagonally through the existing beadwork for several rows, and snip the excess thread close to the work.

START A NEW THREAD (blue line) by weaving diagonally through the existing beadwork for several rows. Stitch through 2 beads in a circle at least twice and weave diagonally through the existing beadwork to exit the last bead exited before ending the thread. String 1 bead (shown in green) and continue stitching.

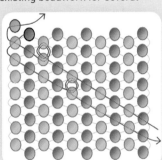

TUBULAR PEYOTE STITCH

This peyote-stitch variation is stitched in the round and is used to make bezels, ropes, and to cover objects.

1 String an even number of beads, leaving a 6" (15.2cm) tail. Tie a square knot to form a circle. This makes up the first and second rounds.

2 String 1 bead, skip the next bead in the original circle, and pass through the following bead; repeat to the end of the circle. (TUBULAR PEYOTE FIGURE 1).

3 Step up for the next round by passing through the first bead added in the row (TUBULAR PEYOTE FIGURE 2).

4 String 1 bead and pass through the next bead from the previous round; repeat to the end of the round (TUBULAR PEYOTE FIGURE 3). Step up for the next round by passing through the first bead added in the current round.

5 Repeat Step 4 to the desired length.

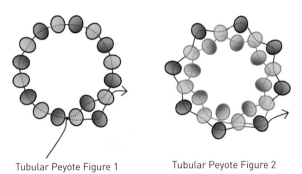

Tubular Peyote Figure 1   Tubular Peyote Figure 2

Tubular Peyote Figure 3

LADDER STITCH

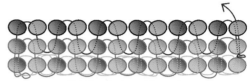

Ladder stitch makes a straight line of beads whose sides touch. It's one way to begin herringbone and brick stitch.

1 Attach a stop bead (see *Stop Bead*, page 134) to a comfortable length of thread. String 2 beads and pass through them again so the beads sit side by side (LADDER STITCH FIGURE 1).

2 String 1 bead and pass through the previous bead and the bead just added, manipulating the beads so their sides touch (LADDER STITCH FIGURE 2).

3 Repeat Step 2 to desired length; weave in excess thread (LADDER STITCH FIGURE 3) or continue in herringbone or brick stitch.

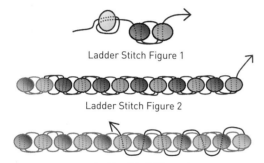

Ladder Stitch Figure 1

Ladder Stitch Figure 2

Ladder Stitch Figure 3

HERRINGBONE STITCH

Herringbone stitch results in beadwork with a graceful drape. It looks great on its own and works well as a surface for embellishing.

1 Ladder-stitch an even number of beads (see *Ladder Stitch*, above) (FLAT HERRINGBONE FIGURE 1).

2 String 2 beads and pass down through the second-to-last bead of the ladder-stitched strip and up through the next bead; repeat to the end of the row. Turn around by looping under the threads of the ladder-stitched strip (FLAT HERRINGBONE, FIGURE 2)

3 String 2 beads, skip 1 bead of the previous row, pass down through the next, and up through the following; repeat across the row. Turn around by looping around the threads between the previous 2 rows (FLAT HERRINGBONE, FIGURE 3).

4 Repeat Step 3 to the desired length.

Flat Herringbone Figure 1

Flat Herringbone Figure 2

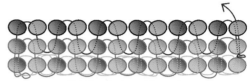

Flat Herringbone Figure 3

ENDING AND STARTING THREAD IN HERRINGBONE STITCH

It's important to maintain the herringbone thread path as you end and start threads in this stitch:

END THE THREAD (red line) by adding the final beads (shown as a green and pink pair), loop around existing threads between the previous 2 rows, pass back up through 1 row, down through 2 rows, and up through 2 rows. Repeat to the edge of the beadwork. Trim the thread close to the work.

START A NEW THREAD (blue line) by repeating the herringbone thread path through 2 rows of existing beadwork. Repeat to the edge of the beadwork. Loop around existing threads at the edge and pass up through the edge beads to exit from the last bead added to continue.

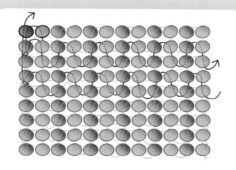

TUBULAR NETTING

Tubular netting is worked in the round, yielding a flexible, lacy beaded rope. It looks great as is or is prime for further embellishment. The following instructions describe three-bead netting, but you can work with any odd number of beads in each stitch—just pass through and step up through the middle bead of each net.

1 String beads in a multiple of 3, leaving a 6" (15.2cm) tail. Tie a square knot to form a circle and pass through the first bead strung.

2 String 3 beads, skip 3 beads of the original circle, and pass through the fourth (TUBULAR NETTING FIGURE 1) repeat around the circle. Step up for the next round by passing through the first 2 beads added in the round (TUBULAR NETTING FIGURE 2)

3 Repeat Step 2 to the desired length (TUBULAR NETTING FIGURE 3).

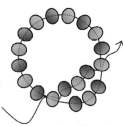

Tubular Netting Figure 1

Tubular Netting Figure 2

Tubular Netting Figure 3

ENDING AND STARTING THREAD WITH NETTING

It's easy to end and start threads within netting as the knots easily hide away in adjacent bead holes.

END THE THREAD (red line) by adding the final 3 beads (shown in a pink/green/pink set), tying an overhand knot around existing threads between beads, and passing through 2 more beads; repeat 3 times. Trim the thread close to the work.

START A NEW THREAD (blue line) by weaving through beads at least 4 rows back, passing through 3 beads, tying an overhand knot around existing threads between beads, and passing up through 2 beads; repeat 3 times and continue to bead.

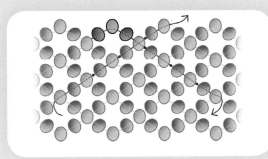

RIGHT-ANGLE WEAVE

Single-needle right-angle weave is a versatile stitch with a multitude of variations. The woven fabric is made up of boxes, or "units," of beads that sit in right angles to one another; each stitch alternates between a clockwise and counterclockwise thread path. It's not always the most intuitive stitch to do, but it may be mastered with concentration.

1 ROW 1 Work 4-bead units in a figure-eight thread path:

Unit 1 String 4 beads, leaving a 6" (15.2cm) tail. Tie a knot to form a circle. Pass through the first bead. (**RAW EVEN FIGURE 1**). String 3 beads and pass through the bead you last exited from the previous unit and the first 2 beads just added (**RAW EVEN FIGURE 2**).

RAW Figure 1

Unit 3 String 3 beads and pass through the bead you last exited from the previous unit and the first 2 beads just added (**RAW FIGURE 3**).

Units 4 and on Repeat Units 2 and 3 to desired even-unit length; when adding the last unit pass through the bead you last exited from the previous unit and the first bead just added to make the turnaround for the next row (**RAW EVEN FIGURE 4**).

RAW Even Figure 2

RAW Even Figure 3

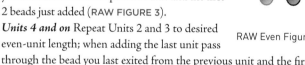

RAW Even Figure 4

2 ROW 2 Work 4-bead units incorporating the top beads from Row 1 in each unit:

Unit 1 String 3 beads and pass through the bead you last exited from the previous unit, the first 3 beads just added, and the top bead of the next unit from the previous row (**RAW EVEN FIGURE 5**).

Unit 2 String 2 beads and pass through the bead you last exited from the previous unit, the top bead of the unit from the previous row, and the first bead just added (**RAW EVEN FIGURE 6**).

Unit 3 String 2 beads and pass through the top bead of the following unit from the previous row, the bead you last exited from the previous unit, the 2 beads just added, and the top bead of the unit from the previous row (**RAW EVEN FIGURE 7**).

Units 4 and on Alternate Units 2 and 3 to the row's end. For the last unit, pass through the bead last exited from the previous unit, the top bead of the last unit from the previous row, and the 2 beads just added (**RAW EVEN FIGURE 8**).

3 ROW 3 Work 4-bead units incorporating the top beads from Row 2 in each unit:

Unit 1 String 3 beads and pass through the bead you last exited from the previous unit and the first bead just added (**RAW EVEN FIGURE 9**).

Unit 2 String 2 beads and pass through the top bead of the next unit from the previous row, the bead you last exited from the previous unit, the 2 beads just added, and the top bead of the following unit from the previous row (**RAW EVEN FIGURE 10**).

RAW Even Figure 5

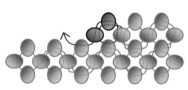

RAW Even Figure 6

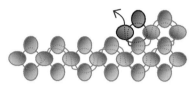

RAW Even Figure 7

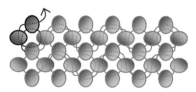

RAW Even Figure 8

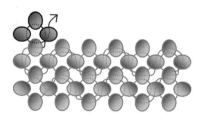

RAW Even Figure 9

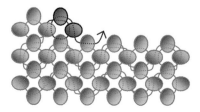

RAW Even Figure 10

Unit 3 String 2 beads and pass through the bead last exited from previous unit, the top bead of the next unit from the previous row, and the first bead just added (**RAW EVEN FIGURE 11**).

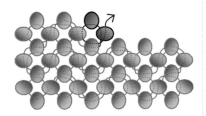

RAW Even Figure 11

Units 4 and on Repeat Units 2 and 3 to the row's end. For the last unit, string 2 beads and pass through the top bead of the final unit from the previous row, the bead you last exited from the previous unit, and the first bead just added (**RAW EVEN FIGURE 12**).

4 Repeat Steps 2 and 3 to the desired length.

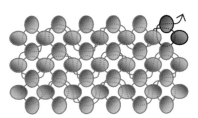

RAW Even Figure 12

ODD-COUNT RIGHT-ANGLE WEAVE

Working a length of right-angle weave with an odd number of units is similar to working one with an even number of units. The difference is that the final turnaround of each completed row and the first stitch of each new row are done in the opposite direction that you would finish and begin even-numbered rows. Just work the rows accordingly, keeping in mind that each unit will alternate clockwise and counterclockwise thread paths.

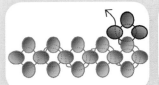
Row 2, first stitch

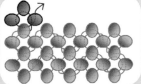
Row 3, first stitch

ENDING AND STARTING THREAD IN RIGHT-ANGLE WEAVE

Follow the existing right-angle weave thread path to end and start new threads, tying knots between beads and pulling tightly on the thread to hide the knots inside the bead holes

END THE THREAD (red line) by adding the final 2 beads, tying an overhand knot around existing threads between beads, and passing through 1 bead; repeat 3 times. Trim the thread close to the work.

START A NEW THREAD (blue line) by passing through beads at least 3 rows back, tying an overhand knot around existing threads between beads, and passing through 1 bead; repeat 3 times. Weave through the beads to exit from the proper starting point.

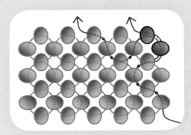

QUADRUPLE HELIX

This looping technique works up into a spiraling tube. Rather than passing through beads to secure them in place, beads are added by hooking over existing threads. The method presented here utilizes a traditional start that requires the 16-bead ring to be knotted extremely tight without any space between the beads. The project *Pacific Waves* (page 18) offers an entirely different start method. A doubled thread thickly coated with beeswax goes a long way in keeping the initial ring extremely tight.

1 START RING. String 16 beads, leaving a 6" (15.2cm) tail. Tie a knot to form an extremely tight ring. Pass through the first 4 beads (QUADRUPLE HELIX FIGURE 1).

Quadruple Helix Figure 1

2 ROUND 1. Work 5-bead loops off of the Start Ring:

Loop 1 String 5 beads, pass down through the center of the Start Ring, and loop around the thread between the third and fourth Start Ring beads (QUADRUPLE HELIX FIGURE 2).

Quadruple Helix Figure 2

Loops 2–4 String 5 beads, pass down through the center of the Start Ring, and loop around the thread between the fourth and fifth Start Ring beads (QUADRUPLE HELIX FIGURE 3). Repeat 2 more times.

Quadruple Helix Figure 3

3 Work continuous spiral rounds by stringing 5 beads, passing down through the 5-bead loop above the one just created, and catching the thread between the third and fourth beads of the adjacent loop (QUADRUPLE HELIX FIGURE 4). Repeat to the desired length.

4 Finish by passing back through the last 2 beads added. String 2 beads and pass through 2 beads from the next loop; repeat 3 times. Weave through the final 16-bead ring twice to reinforce.

Quadruple Helix Figure 4

ENDING AND STARTING THREAD IN QUADRUPLE HELIX

The tricky thing about ending and starting threads with this technique is that since the loops are tied down, your beads can ravel if you haven't properly secured the thread.

END THE THREAD by adding the final 5-bead loop, passing back through all 5 of the beads just added, and passing up through 3 spine beads. Tie a knot around the existing thread between beads, pass through 2 more beads, and pull tight to hide the knot; repeat 3 times. Trim the thread close to the work.

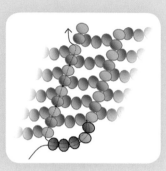

START A NEW THREAD by weaving through 9 beads back on the spine. Pass through 3 beads, tie a knot around the existing thread between beads, pass through 2 beads, and pull tight to hide the knot; repeat 3 times. Weave through beads to begin at the point where the last loop was caught over the thread.

JEFFREY JAY LUHN

About the Author

Rachel Nelson-Smith is a master beadweaver whose work is filled with bold sculptural shapes, vibrant colors, and is infused with her unique combination of fabrication techniques. Her work has been displayed at galleries and museums, including Convergence, Pismo Bead Invitational, Lux Center for the Arts, and the Santa Cruz County Building. Her original pieces have appeared in *Bead & Button* and *Bead Style* magazines as well as *Masters: Beadweaving, Not Your Mama's Beading,* and *Marcia DeCoster's Beaded Opulence.*

Rachel works a dual focus, bringing inspiration to new beaders through basic techniques as well as encouraging personal exploration of improvisational seed-bead stitching and wirework. Since 1996, Rachel has offered basic to advanced workshops in the California Bay Area. Since 2005, she has taught and spoken at national bead shows, including the *Bead & Button* Show, as well as at bead stores and bead societies.

Acknowledgments

That my voice now comes to you can be attributed to those who believed in and helped me from the beginning. Among these people who I'm so fortunate to share time and space are family, friends, and women who work with beads.

Thank you to mom, Maud Pruiett, for believing in me and Mitch Pruiett for coaching and supporting me like I was your own. To my husband, Colin Smith, this accomplishment is possible through your belief in me. Special thanks to Winny Stockwell, Lanny Hendriks, Ellen Gates, and Vicky and Wayne Smith for your support and encouragement. To Mary Vervoort, thank you for feeding my soul. To Jenny Leech, thank you for all time spent discussing my work and dreaming with me.

Related only by our love for beads, these women were instrumental in finding my voice: Sue Mahan, Susan Kazarian, Lisa Niven-Kelly, Toni Yamamoto, and Beth McGuire. To my assistant and sample maker, Liz Penn, thank you for adding clarity and for your beautifully made samples.

To Sharilyn Miller, thank you so much for making the connection. To Tricia Waddell, Rebecca Campbell, Leigh Trotter, Pamela Norman, Joe Coca, Connie Poole, Ann Swanson, and Katherine Jackson, congratulations on another beautiful publication. To Jean Campbell, your editing is supernatural, I've been very fortunate to work with you.

To my fans and you, dear reader, thank you for your support. Bead true. — *Rachel Nelson-Smith*

Shopping Guide

When designing each project, I use sterling silver or copper wire, Swarovski crystals, Japanese seed beads, findings, chain, stringing materials, and glass buttons usually found in local bead stores. Kits including everything needed to create each project as shown are available at www.rachelnelsonsmith.com.

KITS

Rachel Nelson-Smith
PO Box 8331
Santa Cruz, CA 95061
rachelnelsonsmith.com
(408) 348-7003

BEAD SHOPS

The Beading Frenzy
1001 S. El Camino Real
San Mateo, CA 94402
thebeadingfrenzy.com
(650) 347-BEAD

San Gabriel Bead Company
325 E. Live Oak Ave.
Arcadia, CA 91006
beadcompany.com
(626) 614-0014

Creative Castle
2321 Michael Dr.
Newbury Park, CA 91320-3233
creativecastle.com
(805) 499-1377

3 Beads & a Button
20680 Stevens Creek Blvd.
Cupertino, CA 95014
3beads.com
(408) 366-BEAD

Bead It
1325 Pacific Ave.
Santa Cruz, CA 95060
beaditinc.com
(831) 479-0779

Beads By Blanche
106 N. Washington Ave.
Bergenfield, NJ 07621
beadsbyblanche.com
(201) 385-6225

Bead Haven
925 S. Main St. E-1
Frankenmuth, MI 48734
beadhaven.com
(989) 652-3566

U Bead It
2525 Yorktown Ave.
Sacramento, CA 95821
ubeaditsacramento.com
(916) 488-BEAD

Fusion Beads
3830 Stone Wy. N.
Seattle, WA 98103
fusionbeads.com
(206) 782-4595

Out on a Whim
121 E. Cotati Ave.
Cotati, CA 94931
whimbeads.com
(707) 664-8343

Beyond Beadery
PO Box 460
Rollinsville, CO 80474
beayondbeadery.com
(800) 840-5548

Bead Cats
PO Box 2840
Wilsonville, OR 97070
beadcats.com
(503) 625-BEAD

Index

INDEX

Design and Create Exceptional Jewelry
with these inspiring resources from Interweave

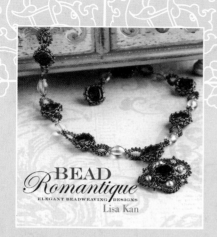

Bead Romantique
Elegant Beadweaving Designs
LISA KAN
ISBN 978-1-59668-046-3
$24.95

Mastering Beadwork
A Comprehensive Guide to Off-Loom Techniques
CAROL HUBER CYPHER
ISBN 978-1-59668-013-5
$24.95

Beader's Companion
Expanded and Updated
JUDITH DURANT
JEAN CAMPBELL
ISBN 978-1-931499-92-7
$19.95

BEADWORK

INSPIRED DESIGNS FOR THE PASSIONATE BEADER

A magazine for beaders who love captivating projects, smart designs, and user-friendly patterns.

beadworkmagazine.com

Are You Beading Daily?

Join BeadingDaily.com, an online community that shares your passion for beading. What do you get? A free e-newsletter, free projects, a daily blog, project store, galleries, a technical glossary and resources, new-product announcements, event updates, and more.

interweavestore.com